Kickoff Upgrade

**Berufsfachschule
Nordrhein-Westfalen**

von
David Christie

Ernst Klett Verlag
Stuttgart · Leipzig

Kickoff Upgrade

Berufsfachschule
Nordrhein-Westfalen

Autor: David Christie, Oxford
Beraterin: Ute Schönenberg–Beyer, Meerbusch

Werkübersicht:

Kickoff Foundation Nordrhein-Westfalen Schülerbuch, Englisch für die Ausbildungsvorbereitungsschule/ Berufsfachschule, 978-3-12-808290-5
Kickoff Foundation Nordrhein-Westfalen Workbook mit Lösungsheft, 978-3-12-808293-6
Kickoff Upgrade Nordrhein-Westfalen Schülerbuch, Englisch für die Berufsfachschule, 978-3-12-808291-2
Kickoff Upgrade Nordrhein-Westfalen Workbook mit Lösungsheft, 978-3-12-808294-3
Kickoff Nordrhein-Westfalen Lehrerhandbuch inkl. Digitalem Lehrer-Service mit Medien-DVD-ROM + Lehrer-Audio-CDs (2), 978-3-12-808292-9

1. Auflage   1 ⁶ | 21

Alle Drucke dieser Auflage sind unverändert und können im Unterricht nebeneinander verwendet werden.
Die letzte Zahl bezeichnet das Jahr des Druckes.
Das Werk und seine Teile sind urheberrechtlich geschützt. Jede Nutzung in anderen als den gesetzlich zugelassenen Fällen bedarf der vorherigen schriftlichen Einwilligung des Verlages. Hinweis § 52 a UrhG: Weder das Werk noch seine Teile dürfen ohne eine solche Einwilligung eingescannt und in ein Netzwerk eingestellt werden. Dies gilt auch für Intranets von Schulen und sonstigen Bildungseinrichtungen. Fotomechanische oder andere Wiedergabeverfahren nur mit Genehmigung des Verlages.
Im Lehrwerk befinden sich ausschließlich fiktive Internet-Adressen, die deshalb auch mit ww#. beginnen anstatt wie üblich mit www.
Die im Buch abgedruckten Mediencodes führen zu interaktiven Zusatzübungen und Downloads auf www.klett.de.
Die Mediencodes leiten ausschließlich zu optionalen Unterrichtsmaterialien, sie unterliegen nicht dem staatlichen Zulassungsverfahren.

© Ernst Klett Verlag GmbH, Stuttgart 2014. Alle Rechte vorbehalten. www.klett.de

Projektleitung: Karin Altrichter
Redaktion: Chris Caridia, London
Herstellung: Sarah Ganser
Satz und Gestaltung: Marion Köster, Stuttgart
Umschlaggestaltung: KOMA AMOK, Kunstbüro für Gestaltung, Stuttgart
Illustrationen: Uwe Alfer, Waldbreitbach; Tanja Kischel, München; Jeongsook Lee, Heidelberg
Reproduktion: Meyle + Müller Medien-Management, Pforzheim
Druck: Firmengruppe APPL, aprinta druck, Wemding

Printed in Germany
ISBN 978-3-12-808291-2

Vorwort

Das neue 2-bändige **Kickoff** Nordrhein-Westfalen entspricht komplett dem Lehrplan der Ausbildungsvorbereitungsschule und der Berufsfachschule, Typ I und II in Nordrhein-Westfalen.

— Durch die Aufteilung in 2 Bände kann **Kickoff** – je nach Schulart – folgendermaßen eingesetzt werden:

Kickoff-Band	Schulart	Bildungsziel	Sprachniveau
Kickoff Foundation	Ausbildungsvorbereitungsschule Berufsfachschule Typ I (erstes Jahr)	nachgeholter oder qualifizierter Hauptschulabschluss	Foundation: A2
Kickoff Upgrade	Berufsfachschule Typ I (zweites Jahr) Berufsfachschule Typ II	Qualifizierter Realschulabschluss	Upgrade: B1

— Noch übersichtlicher durch das komplett überarbeitete Layout.
— Zahlreiche Differenzierungsmöglichkeiten zur individuellen Förderung durch neue Texte und Aufgaben mit unterschiedlichem Schwierigkeitsgrad (leicht – mittel – schwer) auf den selektiv ansteuerbaren *More please!*-Seiten.
— Zahlreiche inhaltliche Erweiterungen:
    – Viele zusätzliche Texte und Hörverständnisaufgaben
    – 7 neue Videos zum Training des Seh-/Hörverstehens
    – Alle *Skills* werden mittels *Skills files* ausführlich dargestellt.
    – Berufsspezifische Vertiefung durch *Job pages* im Anhang.
— Vertieftes Vokabular- und Grammatiktraining:
    Kickoff Foundation Workbook
    Kickoff Upgrade Workbook
— Im Preis bereits dabei: neues, interaktives Vokabeltraining online und zahlreiche Downloads durch Eingabe von **Kickoff**-Codes auf www.klett.de.

Lernhilfen und Symbole:

Am Ende von Unit 4 kann ich:	Lernziele des Lehrplans
Tips and tricks!	Sprachtipps für deutsche Lerner
Hier und dort	Interkulturelles
→ (Vokabel)	Die wichtigsten Vokabeln auf der Seite auf einen Blick
→ More please!	Hinweis auf die Differenzierungsseiten
Video Lounge	authentische Videos
A2.27	Audioverweis
V4	Videoverweis
→ Grammar	Verweis auf die Grammatik
P, M, I, R	Produktion, Mediation, Interaktion oder Rezeption
2se2hk	Vokabeltraining online über www.klett.de und Audio-Download (MP3)
▵	Differenzierung nach unten
▲	Differenzierung nach oben

| Topics | Language | Check-out activities / Video Lounge |

Unit 1 Get ready for work! — 6

- vocational colleges in England
- choosing a career
- talking about yourself, your college, and your future plans

revision of:
- simple present
- present continuous
- simple past
- *will* future
- *must / mustn't / have to / don't have to*

- posting a message on the internet
- introducing yourself in a short talk
- **Video lounge** Choosing a career

Unit 2 Travelling for work — 16

- talking about travel
- how airports work
- understanding hotel brochures
- checking in at a hotel

- relative pronouns *who, which, where*
- relative sentences

- writing a holiday postcard
- role-playing travel situations
- **Video lounge** Welcome back

Unit 3 A visit to a company — 26

- understanding companies and processes
- introducing yourself and others politely

- adjectives and adverbs
- adverbs of manner

- writing a report
- making a poster about a company
- **Video lounge** Plans

Unit 4 Global business — 36

- living in a globalised world
- the production and global distribution of goods
- the 'good' and 'bad' sides of globalisation

- simple present passive
- simple past passive

- a class survey
- making a poster about a process / an aspect of globalisation
- **Video lounge** How was your visit?

Unit 5 A month in New Zealand — 46

- New Zealand: country, people, history
- using polite language to deal with everyday situations

- present perfect with *since / for*

- writing a text to describe Germany
- **Video lounge** Goodbye

| Topics | Language | Check-out activities / Video Lounge |

Unit 6 Apprenticeships — 56

- apprenticeships in England
- applying for an apprenticeship
- an interview for an apprenticeship

- *if*-sentences type 2

- writing a CV
- describing a cartoon
- **Video lounge**
  Applying for a job

Unit 7 Starting work — 66

- working as a retail assistant
- tips for the first days at work

- verbs + infinitive / verbs + *ing*-form

- making a mindmap
- making a conversation about a job
- **Video lounge**
  Starting a new job

Partner files / Job Pages / Test — 76

Partner files   77
Job pages: 78
> Phoning at work (Unit 1)
> Preparing for a meeting (Unit 2)
> Business correspondence 1: an enquiry (Unit 3)
> Business correspondence 2: an offer (Unit 4)
> Business correspondence 3: an order (Unit 5)
> Business correspondence 4: a complaint (Unit 6)
> Understanding advertisements (Unit 7)
Test   92

Anhang Grammar summary / Skills files / Vocabulary — 96

Grammar summary   97
Skills files   107
Unitbegleitendes Vokabular   120
Alphabetisches Vokabular   131
Abbildungsnachweis   135

Unit 1
Get ready for work!

Check-in | Training | More please! | Check-out

1 Hi! I'm a student

P, I **A** Describe the picture at the top opposite. Make notes with the phrases below, then compare with a partner and report to the class. → Skills 13

In the picture there are … people.
They seem to be in …
In the foreground / background you can see …
On the right / the left …
I think one (of the people) is a …
The other (person) is maybe …
They're …ing (looking at? talking about? …?)
Perhaps …

Hier und dort
Sowohl in den USA als auch in Großbritannien und in einigen anderen englischsprachigen Ländern findet die Berufsbildung auf einem *college* statt, und die Lernenden sind *students*. In *Kickoff* benutzen wir durchgehend diese Wörter für dich und deine Schule.

P, I **B** The young man in the picture is Colin and opposite you can see his college. Read what Colin says below and answer the questions.

A 2.1

> Hi! My name's Colin Williams and I live in the UK – in a town in the north of England called Bolton. I'm 17 years old and I'm a student at a vocational college. I started my course last year, so now I'm in my second year at college. If all goes well, I'll finish at the end of this year and then I want to become an IT technician.

1. Where does Colin come from and where is he a student?
2. When did he start his course and when will he finish?
3. What job does Colin want to have after college?

P, I **C** Now YOU! Say 'hi' to your class and give some facts about yourself.

→ (to be a) student   → (vocational) college   → course
→ to become (a …)

Am Ende von Unit 1 habe ich:
— Grundlagen der Grammatik wiederholt,
— berufsspezifische Vokabeln gelernt.

Unit 1 Get ready for work! 7

Check-in Training More please! Check-out

2 At college in England

R, P A2.2

A Read about vocational education in England and answer the questions below. Write full sentences for your answers.

In England, young people must be in full-time education until they are 18. Some stay at school, but many others leave school at 16 and go to a vocational college – called a College of Further
5 Education, or usually just an FE college.

FE students usually stay at their college for two years. Classes are normally full-time, five days a week. Classes start at around 9 am and finish around 4 pm and because students are at college all day, there is always a cafeteria where they can eat at lunchtime.

10 So what do students learn at college? That depends. FE colleges in Britain are often very large and offer many different kinds of courses, but many 16- to 18-year-olds choose a course at the beginning of their two years which trains them for a job – for example, a 'hairdressing course' or one to become a construction
15 worker or a fashion designer. Colin Williams wants to be a computer technician, so he is on an IT course. Many classes are practical, so colleges usually have workshops for mechanics, kitchens for trainee chefs, and computer rooms for students like Colin. In the picture, one of Colin's friends, Michael, is working
20 in the college's woodworking workshop. He is training to be a carpenter and at the moment he is cutting a piece of wood. His teacher is watching and helping.

1 What two different things can British school pupils do at the age of 16?
2 Why do British FE colleges usually have a cafeteria?
3 Name four different kinds of courses for 16- to 18-year-olds at a typical FE college.
4 Where does Colin work a lot of the time each day when he is at college?
5 Who is the person in the foreground of the picture at the bottom? What is he doing at the moment?

→ full-time education   → an FE college   → (to be on) a course
→ That depends   → to train (to be sth)

R, I, P
A 2.3

B Listen to Colin again. Are the sentences below true or false? Write down 'T' or 'F' and correct the false sentences. Compare with a partner, then report to the class. → Skills 13

1. Colin was born in Bolton.
   F. He was born in …
2. He came to live in Bolton when he was 11.
3. His family moved there because his mum got a job.
4. He likes Bolton now but he was unhappy at first.
5. Colin was good at most subjects at school.
6. He chose the IT course because his dad helped him a lot.
7. Colin is in his first year at college in Bolton.
8. He likes college because he feels like an adult and not a little kid.

R, P **C** Work in small groups to do the tasks below, then report to the class.

1. Copy the chart below and fill in the missing forms of the verb *to work*.

	The simple present	The present continuous	The simple past
I	work	?	?
he / she / it	?	is working	?
we	?	?	worked
you	?	?	?
they	?	?	?

2. Check your answers in class, then find two or three examples of each tense in the text on page 8 and task B on this page. Remember! The simple past forms of some verbs are irregular – for example, *eat → ate* or *go → went* – and some of the verbs in task B are like this!
3. Look at the information about these tenses at the back of your book, then explain why your sentences are examples of the simple past, present continuous or simple past.

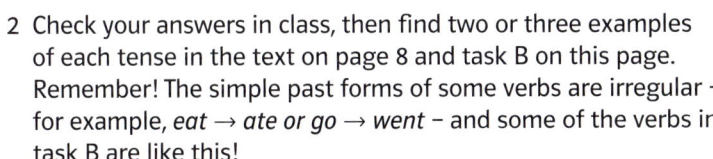

→ to go to school → funny → (to have) a sense of humour
→ to decide (to do sth) → an adult (↔ a kid)

Unit 1 Get ready for work! 9

Check-in | **Training** | More please! | Check-out

3 Choosing a career

Choosing a career is never easy and before you decide, it is a good idea to get information about lots of different jobs. One way to do this is to look at some 'job profiles' – for example, online. You can see two profiles below.

JOB PROFILE NURSERY WORKER

Description
Nursery workers work with babies and small children in a nursery.

Tasks
- feeding and changing babies
- organising play activities
- reading stories
- taking children out in groups
- making sure that children are safe and well
- talking to parents

Skills
Nursery workers have to:
- be interested in children
- know about safety and hygiene
- work well in a team
- be responsible and caring

JOB PROFILE ADMINISTRATIVE ASSISTANT

Description
Administrative assistants work in an office and it is their job to make sure that day-to-day life in the office runs smoothly.

Tasks
- opening letters
- answering the telephone
- looking after visitors
- typing letters and other documents
- receiving and sending emails
- photocopying and printing documents

Skills
Administrative assistants have to:
- like working in an office
- be accurate and well-organised
- be good with computers
- work well in a team
- communicate well with people

→ job profile   → task   → skill(s)
→ to type (documents)   → to communicate (with sb)
→ (to be) responsible

R, P **A** Chloe Taylor is 16 and a pupil at a school in England. She wants to leave school this year and go to an FE college, but can't decide what career she would like to choose. She is looking at the two job profiles opposite. Complete the sentences about the two jobs.

1 If Chloe becomes an administrative assistant, she will work in an ... (where?).
2 If she becomes a nursery worker, she will work in a ...
3 If she becomes a ... , she will work with children.
4 She won't work with children if she becomes a ... (she will work with adults).
5 Chloe likes computers and if she becomes a ... she will type documents and send emails.
6 But Chloe also loves playing with her little sister and if she becomes a ... , she will organise play activities.

P **B** Now complete the table below and write three more sentences about the two jobs on page 10 like those in task A above.

If-sentences type 1	→ More please **H, I**
if + simple present	will
If she becomes a nursery worker,	she will (won't) …

R, P **C** Compare the two jobs again. Look at the Tips and tricks box and then say if the sentences below are true or false. Correct the false sentences. → More please! J

1 Admin assistants have to be good with computers. T
2 Admin assistants have to be good with children. F
   Admin assistants … with children.
3 Admin assistants have to like working in an office.
4 Nursery workers have to like working in an office.
5 Nursery workers have to make children unhappy.
6 Admin assistants have to make lots of mistakes in documents.
7 Admin assistants and nursery workers both have to work well in a team.
8 And they both have to feed and change babies.

Tips and tricks
Vorsicht!
you have to (must) = du **musst**
you don't have to = du **musst nicht** (brauchst nicht)
you mustn't = du **darfst nicht**

→ administrative (admin) assistant   → nursery (worker)
→ to organise sth   → to make a mistake

4 More please!

A The simple present → Grammar 1

Complete the sentences with the correct forms of the verbs in brackets (...).

1 (live) I *live* in Germany.
2 (live) Colin ... in England.
3 (go) He ... to an FE college in Bolton.
4 (go) Lots of young people in Britain ... to an FE college.
5 (start) I usually ... my lessons at 8.30.
6 (start) Colin ... at nine.
7 (eat) At lunchtime, he ... in the cafeteria.
8 (finish) And he ... college at around 4 pm.

> **Tips and tricks**
> Nicht vergessen:
> *he / she / it* das '*s*' muss mit!

B The present continuous → Grammar 2

Complete these sentences with the present continuous forms of the verbs in brackets (...).

1 (work) At the moment, Colin *is working* in the computer room.
2 (learn) I ... English at the moment.
3 (do) What ... you ... at the moment?
4 (train) In this picture, Colin's friend Michael ... to be a carpenter.
5 (cut) He ... a piece of wood right now.
6 (cut) These students are in the college's hairdressing salon. They ... hair.

The first year hairdressing class wanted volunteers in the salon.

C The simple present / the present continuous → Grammar 1, 2

Choose the correct forms of the verbs a or b.

1 Colin Williams a) lives   b) is living in England.
2 He a) wants b) is wanting to be a computer technician.
3 I a) live b) am living in Germany.
4 Right now, Colin a) works   b) is working in the computer room at college.
5 Right now, I a) do   b) am doing this exercise.
6 You can see two people in this picture. They a) talk b) are talking.
7 Hi, George. What a) do you do   b) are you doing at the moment?
  – I a) listen   b) am listening to music on my smartphone.
8 In England, college students usually a) have   b) are having lunch in the cafeteria.

D The simple present / the present continuous → Grammar 1, 2

Complete the sentences with the correct form of the verb in brackets (. . .).

1 (come) Colin Williams *comes* from Bolton in the north of England.
2 (not/come) I ... from England, I'm German.
3 (stay) In England, young people ... at school or college until they are 18.
4 (have) English FE colleges usually ... rooms and workshops where students can do practical lessons.
5 (work/cut) In this picture, some students ... in the college's hairdressing salon. Right now, they ... hair.
6 (do) At the moment, I ... this exercise.
7 (do/listen) Hi Maria. What ... at the moment? – I ... to music on my smartphone.

E The simple present with *usually/often/...* → Grammar 1

Write the sentences again with the adverb in the correct place in the sentences.

1 (usually) I come to college by bike.
I usually come to college by bike.
2 (sometimes) But in the winter, I come by bus.
3 (often) British students have lunch in the college cafeteria.
4 (normally) English FE colleges are very large.
5 (never) I'm late for lessons!
6 (never) And I use my mobile during lessons!

F The simple past → Grammar 3

This is Rebecca. Choose the correct verbs to finish the text about her. Use each verb only once.

Rebecca goes to the FE college in Bolton where Colin is also a student. Rebecca – or 'Becky' to her friends – **(1)** *was born* in Bolton and she **(2)** ... to school there until she **(3)** ... 16. She **(4)** ... the cleverest pupil in her class at school but she **(5)** ... art and being creative. And in her last two years at school she **(6)** ... a great art teacher who **(7)** ... Becky a lot with her ideas. So when she started college, Becky **(8)** ... to do a fashion design course. Her mum and dad also **(9)** ... this was a great idea – they have a small shop in Bolton which sells clothes. Becky loves the course and last year she **(10)** ... a prize for her clothes in a fashion competition.

decided
had
helped
loved
thought
was
wasn't
went
won
was born

Unit 1 Get ready for work!

| Check-in | Training | More please! | Check-out |

P G **The simple past** → Grammar 3

▲ **Complete the sentences with the verbs in brackets. Use the simple past. Be careful! Lots of verbs are irregular.**

1 (be born / go) I *was born* in my hometown and I **...** to school here, too.
2 (be) My favourite subjects at school **...** history and English.
3 (be / visit) One great thing at school **...** a class trip – we **...** London.
4 (see / eat / meet) We **...** lots of famous sights, **...** fish and chips, and **...** some young English people.
5 (leave / start) I **...** school last summer and **...** college two weeks ago.
6 (not be) It **...** easy at first, but I think I'll like it here. We'll see!

   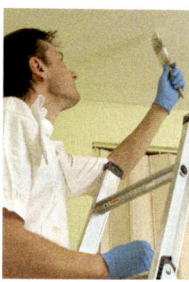 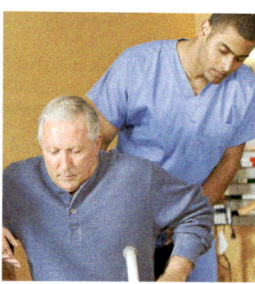 

R H *If*-**Sentences Type 1** → Grammar 9

△ **Look at the job pictures and match the sentence halves below. Use your dictionary for any words you don't know.**

1 If you become a painter and decorator,   a you will repair cars.
2 If you become a mechanic,   b if you become a nurse.
3 You will work in a kitchen   c if you work in an office one day.
4 You will help sick people   d you will work in a shop.
5 If you become a shop assistant,   e you will paint and decorate houses and flats.
6 You will often talk on the phone   f if you become a chef.

P I *If*-**Sentences Type 1** → Grammar 9

▲ **Look at the job pictures above and quickly complete task H. Now choose three pictures and write a sentence about each yourself. Use conditional sentences type 1.**

R J **have to (must) / don't have to / mustn't** → Grammar 8

▲ **Choose the correct forms a or b.**

1 This is a NO SMOKING sign. It means you a) mustn't   b) must smoke here.
2 And this NO PARKING sign means you a) mustn't   b) don't have to park here.
3 I go to college Monday to Friday but I a) mustn't   b) don't have to go at weekends.
4 In Germany we drive on the right. But you a) don't have to   b) mustn't drive on the right in England, Australia or Japan. In these countries you a) mustn't   b) have to drive on the left.

5 Now you

P, I **A** **Work in small groups.**

Copy and complete the table. Then choose one task below:
a You have an internet link with an FE college in England. The students there want to know about you and your college in Germany. Write a short text based on your table.
b Next week you will go to a conference in London for vocational students from around the EU. At the start of the conference, students have to introduce themselves to the others. Write and give a short talk (2–3 minutes) based on your table.

Personal details	(name, age, live in …)
Born?	(where? when?)
School	(where? favourite subjects? favourite teacher?)
College	(where? name? when did you start?)
Daily routine	(lessons, times, lunch, subjects)
Career plans	(want to do after college? Can you give a reason?)

Hello. My name is … I'm and I …/ I was born … I went to school …/

Video Lounge Choosing a career

Maya lives in London. Today, she is at a careers advice centre. You will see two parts of her interview with a woman called Louise Kane. Watch and answer the questions.

Part 1
1 What is Maya's "dream job"?
2 What subjects did she like at school?
3 What activities does she like?
4 What job profile does she look at on the careers database?

Part 2
Maya thinks that to be a hotel manager would be nice, but she will need to train for three years and she thinks that's too long.
1 What does Ms Kane suggest? Where and with what company?
2 What tip does she give Maya at the very end? Why does she say this?

Unit 2
Travelling for work

Check-in | Training | More please! | Check-out

1 Check in!

A Talk in class. How do you travel? Finish the sentences with the best words for you.

1 I ... come to college by bike.
2 In town, I ... travel by bus.
3 I ... travel by tram or S-Bahn.
4 When I go on holiday, I ... travel by plane.

always
often
usually / normally
sometimes
never
hardly ever

Tips and tricks
You go ...
· by bike / train / bus / tram / underground
· by car (or you **drive**)
· by plane (or you **fly**)
· on foot (or you **walk**)

B Herr Kreuger is a businessman. Today, he's on a business trip to London. Right now he's checking in at the check-in desk. Finish the sentences below with *who, which* or *where*.

1 The place ... you check in at an airport is the check-in desk.
2 The man ... is checking in here is Herr Kreuger.
3 The woman ... is helping him is Frau Bliscz. She's a check-in clerk.
4 The document ... she has in her hand is Herr Kreuger's boarding card.

C Finish these sentences in your own words.

1 An airport is a place where ...
2 A businessman or woman is a person who ...
3 A plane is a big machine which ...
4 A ... is ...

→ to check in → (check-in) desk → (check-in) clerk
→ boarding card

Am Ende von Unit 2 kann ich:

— über Reisen, Flughäfen und Hotels sprechen und schreiben,
— Menschen, Sachen und Orte detailliert beschreiben,
— eine Postkarte erstellen.

Unit 2 Travelling for work

| Check-in ✚ Training | More please! | Check-out

2 How an airport works

A Look at the picture of the airport on the next page and read the text below. Then answer the questions.

People who travel by plane from or to an airport (like Herr Kreuger) are passengers. When passengers fly from an airport, they go to DEPARTURES. First, they check in at the check-in desk. The check-in clerk gives them a boarding card. On it,
5 passengers can see the number of the gate where their plane departs.

Next they go through the security check. Here, security officers check people's clothes and their hand baggage. After that, passengers go through the passport check. Passport officers
10 check their passports. Now passengers usually have some time before their plane departs. There are cafés, restaurants and shops where they can eat, drink and buy things.

Finally, passengers get on (or 'board') the plane – and the
15 plane takes off. And when passengers arrive at an airport? Well, they go through the passport check, get their baggage at the baggage reclaim, go through the customs check (where customs officers sometimes check their baggage) – and that's it. Easy!

security check

passport check

B Put these words in the right order under the right heading. You can use some words twice.

departure	arrival
check-in desk	…
…	

cup of coffee
plane
check-in desk
customs
passport check
gate
baggage reclaim

→ passenger   → to depart   → (hand) baggage   → to check   → to arrive at (an airport)

R, P **C** Here are some people, places and things which you find at an airport. What are they? Finish the definitions, then make two more definitions yourself.

1 The security check is the place *where security officers* …
2 A passport officer is a person / someone …
3 A boarding pass is something / a document …

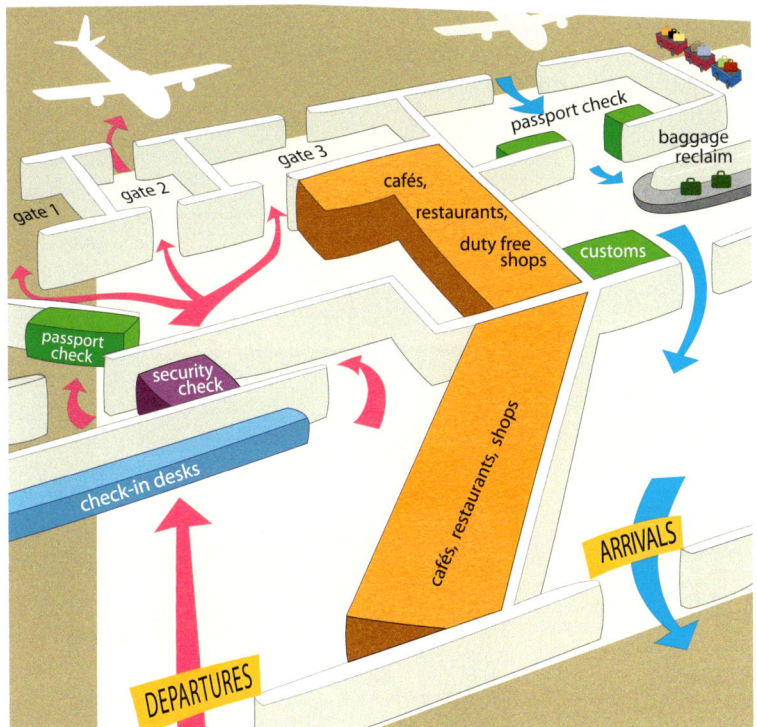

M **D** Your German friend has to fly to the USA tomorrow. It's his/her first time at an airport. Explain in German what he or she has to do at the airport – first here in Germany, then when he/she arrives in the USA.

P **E** Can you give the missing words?

Relativsätze	→ More please **A – C**
People	A pilot is a person / someone … flies a plane.
Things	A plane is a big machine … can fly.
Places	A restaurant is a place … you can eat and drink.

→ departure(s)   → arrival(s)   → baggage reclaim   → duty free (shop)   → customs

Unit 2 Travelling for work

Check-in | **Training** | More please! | Check-out

3 At a hotel

R **A** **Read about Sandra and look at the hotel brochure. Then answer the questions on the next page.**

Sandra Kaiser is from Hamburg in Germany. She has an exciting job. Her company builds roller coasters – the big machines which you often see at theme parks and fairs. Sandra is an electrical technician. She checks and services the electrical equipment on the roller coasters. Her company builds roller coasters around the world, so Sandra often travels in her job and she often stays at hotels. This week, she's at a hotel in the north of England called the River Hotel.

Welcome To The River Hotel

The River Hotel is a quiet, friendly hotel only 10 minutes on foot from the River Towers Theme Park. Ideal for families – children under 10 stay free.

ROOMS
12 single rooms
10 double rooms
10 family rooms (2 adults + 2 children)

All rooms have a bathroom and shower.

FACILITIES
The River Restaurant
Bar
Garden with children's playground
Free parking
TV in all rooms
Wi-Fi Internet connection

Please note that we are a non-smoking hotel.

→ to service (equipment) → to stay at (a hotel) → single / double room → facilities

20

1 Answer the questions about Sandra and her job in full sentences.

a Where's Sandra from?
b What does Sandra's company build?
c What's a roller coaster?
d What's Sandra's job? What work does she do?
e What does Sandra often do in her job? Why?
f Where's Sandra this week?

2 True or false? Note down T or F.

a The hotel has a total of 32 rooms.
b You can walk from the hotel to the *River Towers Theme Park* in 10 minutes.
c You can smoke at the hotel.
d A mum, a dad and three children can stay in a family room.
e Children under 10 don't have to pay for their room.
f Parking at the hotel costs £1.00 a day.
g You can use the internet at the hotel.
h The single rooms at the hotel don't have a bathroom or shower.

Tips and tricks
Adverbien sowie *often*, *always*, *sometimes* stehen immer **vor** einem Vollverb:
*She **often** travels in her job.*

B Sandra is checking in at the hotel. Listen. Find the missing words from the list below.

6 am to 10 am · key · the second floor · registration form · A single room · You're welcome. · 214

Receptionist   Sandra

Hello. How can I help you?
　　　　Hello. My name's Kaiser. K-A-I-S-E-R.
　　　　You have a room for me.
Just a moment. Ah yes, Ms Kaiser. (1) ... for four nights?
　　　　That's right.
Would you fill in the (2) ... for me, please?
　　　　Mmm. Here you are.
Thanks. Here's your (3) ... You're in room (4) ... That's on (5) ...
There's a lift just over there. Breakfast is from (6) ...
in the restaurant over there.
　　　　Great. Thanks very much.
(7) ... Enjoy your stay with us.

C Now YOU. Read the dialogue with a partner. Then change the names, times, room number etc. and make a new dialogue.
→ More please! D – G

→ registration form   → key   → on the second floor   → over there

Unit 2 Travelling for work   **21**

Check-in | Training | **More please!** | Check-out

4 More please!

A Relativsätze → Grammar 12

Make sentences. Write out your sentences in full.

1 A passenger is a person		you check in is the check-in desk.
2 The place in an airport	who	you can get a coffee or other drink.
3 A café is a place	which	flies by plane.
4 A passport is a document	where	you get your baggage when you home.
5 A check-in clerk is someone		you need to travel abroad.
6 The baggage reclaim is		works at a check-in desk.

A passenger is a person who …

B Airport vocabulary

Look at the pictures and give the missing words in the sentences below.

A

B

1 Someone who travels by plane is called a *passenger*.
2 The place where passengers go first (picture A) is the …
3 Here, they get the piece of paper which you can see in picture B. It's called a …
4 Before passengers can board a plane they have to go through a place where people check their clothes and hand luggage (picture C). This place is called the …
5 The people who work here are the …
6 Finally, passengers go to the place where they board their plane. It has a number like A10 or B24 and it's called a …

C

22

C Relativsätze / airport vocabulary → Grammar 12

Look at the pictures on page 22, then complete the sentences below with *who*, *which* or *where* and words you have learned about airports.

1 The person *who* works at the place in picture A is called a ... .
2 For international flights, passengers also need another document ... they have to show at the 'Passkontrolle'. In English, this document is called a ... .
3 There are always places at an airport ... passengers can eat, drink and buy things – ... , ... and ... .
4 When passengers board their plane, how do they know which seat to sit in? Well, they find the seat number ... is on their ... .
5 When passengers arrive at an airport from another country, they get off the plane and then they go to find their baggage. The place ... they do this is called the ... .
6 There is one more thing, too, when you come from another country. People ... are called ... check your baggage when you go through the customs check.

D Hotel vocabulary

Choose the correct words and phrases to finish the sentences.

1 Lots of famous people *stay at* this hotel.
2 The hotel's ... include a swimming pool and fitness room.
3 You don't have to pay for parking here, it's ... .
4 You can use your laptop here because there's an internet ... .
5 Every bathroom has a ... and toilet.
6 When you arrive at a hotel, you have to fill in a ... .
7 Then the ... gives you the ... for your room.

connection facilities receptionist free key registration form shower stay at

E Hotel vocabulary

Below are definitions of some things, places and people in a hotel. What are they? All the words are on pages 20–21.

1 A small metal object which you use to open a door.
2 A form which you fill in when you arrive at a hotel.
3 A place where you sleep. If you are alone, you get a single one of these.
4 The person who welcomes you when you arrive and who checks you into the hotel.
5 The meal which you eat in the morning, probably in the hotel's restaurant.
6 A place in a hotel where you can get an alcoholic drink.

"The room was dirty, the television didn't work, the shower was cold and the food in the restaurant was terrible. Otherwise, did you enjoy your stay?"

M ▲ **F Hotel vocabulary**

In today's world of work everyone travels more and more. One day, you will perhaps have to stay at a hotel in an English-speaking country in your job. So, could you check in? Give the phrases you need below in English.

Receptionist   **You**

Good morning. How can I help you?
         Guten Morgen. Mein Name ist *(Ihr Name)*. Sie haben ein Zimmer für mich für zwei Nächte reserviert.
         Good morning. My …

Just a moment. Ah yes, that's right. A single room for tonight and tomorrow night. Would you fill in this form for me, please?
         Mmm. So, bitte schön.

Thanks. Here's your key. Your room is on the fourth floor.
         Danke. Gibt es einen Aufzug?

Yes, just over there.
         Ah ja, danke. Ich habe Hunger. Haben Sie ein Restaurant?

Yes, it's on the first floor. It's open until 11.00 this evening.
         Klasse. Vielen Dank.

You're welcome. Enjoy your stay with us.

P, I ▲ **G Travel vocabulary**

Work with a partner. Copy the TRAVEL mindmap below, then add 15 more words and phrases yourselves. Report to the class.

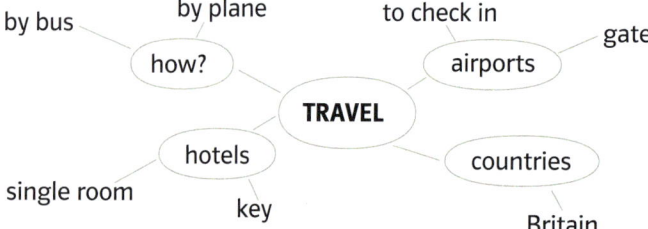

So läuft's besser

Mindmaps sind eine gute Methode, Vokabeln zu sammeln und thematisch zu lernen. In einer Mindmap werden Begriffe rund um ein Thema gesammelt. Mindmaps können einzelne Wörter sowie Redewendungen enthalten. So bekommt man einen tollen Überblick!

R, P ▲ **H Key words**

Find the key words and phrases from pages 17 – 21 below. Choose five and write a sentence with each.

CUSTOMSSINGLEROOMBOARDINGCARDPASSENGERDUTYFREESHOPCHECKINDESKHANDBAGGAGEOVERTHEREFACILITIESTODEPARTBAGGAGERECLAIMONTHESECONDFLOORKEY

5 Now you

A A holiday postcard. You're on holiday. Send a postcard to an American friend. Think of the missing information yourself and finish the postcard below.

> Dear **(1)** ... ,
>
> I'm on holiday in **(2)** ... with **(3)** ... . The weather is **(4)** ... . The hotel where we are is **(5)** ... . Right now I'm **(6)** ... . Yesterday we **(7)** ...
>
> Best wishes, **(8)** ...

B Role-play
1 Work in a small group. Look back at the texts and conversations in this unit. Choose some situations which you think are interesting. They can be at an airport, a hotel, in a shop, in a café, …
2 Take parts and role-play the situations in your group. Then show the class.

Video Lounge Welcome back

Jasmine is a PA (personal assistant) in a company in England. Six months ago, two businessmen from Australia, John Carter and Paul Rogers, visited Jasmine's company and Jasmine looked after them then. Now they are visiting her company again.

A Watch the video.

1 Where are Mr Carter and Mr Rogers when Jasmine meets them?
2 Jasmine asks the men if they have checked in … (what?) OK.
3 What does Mr Rogers give Jasmine? What will she do with it?

B Watch again and find the English for:

Schön dich / Sie wiederzusehen. · Mir geht's gut, danke. Und dir / Ihnen? · Kein Problem. · Vielen Dank! Das ist wirklich sehr nett von dir / Ihnen!

Unit 3
A visit to a company

Check-in | Training | More please! | Check-out

1 A week in England

R, P
A 2.6

A Read the short text below and answer the questions.

Tobias, Patricia, Iris and Melanie are from Germany. They're apprentices in a German chemicals company and all want to be laboratory technicians. This week they're in England with their trainer, Herr Wolf. Right now, they're visiting a company which makes paint. It's called Rolac Paints PLC. They're just arriving at the company. They have an appointment there in a couple of minutes so they're walking quickly.

1 Describe the two pictures opposite. Say who and what you can see, and what's happening.
2 How are the people walking (quickly? slowly? …?) Why?

I, P
B How do you do these things? Finish the sentences for yourself, then compare your answers with a partner and report to the class.

1 In the morning, I usually get up …
   (quite) quickly   (very) slowly

2 I usually get to my lessons …
   punctually   not very punctually

3 I think I speak English …
   (very) well   quite well   OK (satisfactorily)
      not too well   (quite) badly

In the morning, I get up quite quickly, but my partner Klaas …
Klaas and I / We both …

→ company   → apprentice   → PLC   → quickly   → slowly
→ punctually   → (quite) well   → badly

Am Ende von Unit 3 kann ich:
— über Unternehmen schreiben und sprechen,
— andere höflich begrüßen,
— sagen, wie man Dinge macht (schnell, langsam usw.).

Unit 3 A visit to a company 27

Check-in Training More please! Check-out

2 Welcome to Rolac

R **A** Before their visit, the apprentices read a brochure about Rolac Paints PLC. Look at this page from the brochure. Find out:

1. How old is the company?
2. How did the company grow in the 1950s and 60s? How important is it today?
3. Where are the company's head office and main factory?
4. How do many processes in the Rolac factory happen?
5. What different sorts of paint does the company make? What sorts of people buy them?

A 2.7

Welcome to
ROLAC PAINTS PLC

About Rolac and the factory
ROLAC PAINTS started in 1876. In the 1950s and 60s, the company grew very quickly and it is now one of the world's largest manufacturers of paint. Our main factory and our head
5   office are here in England, but we also have factories and offices in the USA, Russia, Australia and China. The factory which you are visiting today is very modern. Many processes happen automatically with computers and robots. But they can't do everything! Over 1,000 people work here, too.

10 **Who uses our paint?**
Rolac makes many different sorts of paint – for people's homes, for buildings, for cars, lorries and tractors – even for bridges. So lots of different people buy our paints, from customers in DIY shops to big companies.

15 Today, you can walk slowly around our factory and see exactly how we make our paints. We are very happy that you are here – enjoy your visit!

P **B** What are the missing forms?

Adjektive	Adverbien → More please A – B
This old bus is very **slow**.	It travels ?
But this new bus is **quick**.	It travels ?
The process is **automatic**.	The process happens ?
Here's an **exact** diagram of the factory.	On it, you can see ? how we make our paints.

→ head office   → factory   → to grow   → manufacturer   → DIY (Do It Yourself) shop

28

C Tobias, Patricia, Iris, Melanie and Herr Wolf are just arriving at Rolac Paints PLC. Ms Roberts, from the company, is waiting for them at the reception desk. Listen, then read the conversation in a group.

Ms Roberts	Herr Wolf? Hello, I'm Christine Roberts.
Herr Wolf	Oh, hello, Ms Roberts. Nice to meet you.
Ms Roberts	Please, call me Christine.
Herr Wolf	And I'm Jan. It's great to be here. Can I introduce our apprentices? This is Melanie Seiler.
Melanie	Nice to meet you.
Herr Wolf	Tobias Schumann.
Tobias	Pleased to meet you, Ms Roberts.
Herr Wolf	And Patricia Schwarz and Iris Büchsel.
Patricia	Nice to meet you.
Iris	Pleased to meet you, Ms Roberts.
Ms Roberts	Nice to meet you all, too. OK. Let's go to the cafeteria. We can have a cup of coffee, then you can look round the factory with me. How's your English by the way?
Apprentices	Mmmm!
Herr Wolf	I think we all speak English quite well but perhaps you can speak slowly for us?
Ms Roberts	Sure. OK, please come this way …

D Now YOU. Work in your groups again. Imagine that you are visiting a company. One of you is a trainer (like Herr Wolf), and one of you is from the company (like Ms Roberts). There are also some apprentices. Write a conversation, then act your conversation for the class. → More please! C

→ to introduce s.o.   → Nice / Pleased to meet you (too).
→ to imagine

Hier und dort
Nice to meet you!
Briten (und Amerikaner) scheinen oft deutlich weniger förmlich zu sein als Deutsche. Z. B. verwenden sie in der Wirtschaft schnell Vornamen. Aber: Warte bis dein Gesprächspartner dir dies anbietet! Die Standardbegrüßung ist *Nice to meet you*, oder *Pleased to meet you* and die Antwort hierauf ist *Nice / Pleased to meet you, too.*

Sich die Hand geben in GB
Briten geben sich seltener die Hand als Deutsche. Es ist in GB nicht üblich, dass sich Freunde und Arbeitskollegen täglich die Hände schütteln.

Unit 3 A visit to a company

Check-in | Training | More please! | Check-out

3 A tour of the factory

R **A** The German group is looking around the factory with Ms Roberts. Here's a plan of the factory. Match the English and the German words.

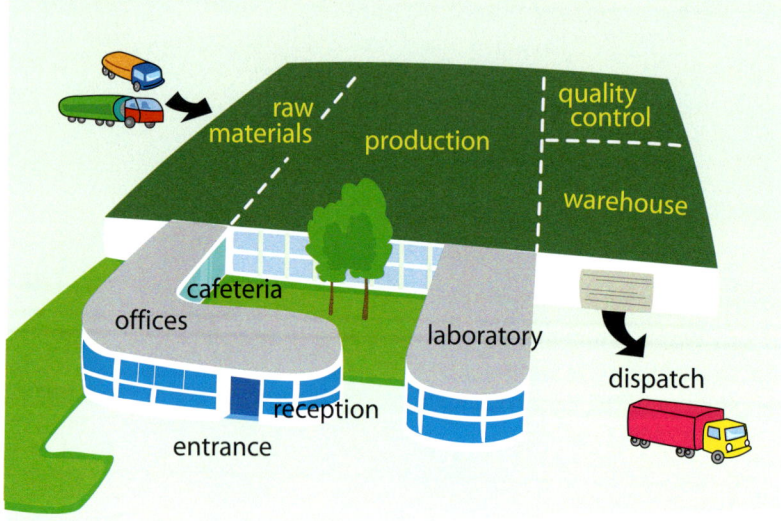

Labor
Büros
Herstellung
Lagerhalle
Eingang
Kantine
Rohstoffe
Rezeption
Abfertigung
Qualitätssicherung

A 2.9

B Now listen to Ms Roberts. Look at the plan above. Which parts of the factory do they visit first, second, third, …?

First they go to …
Then/Next they visit …
After that …
Finally, …

A 2.9

C Listen again. Write down the missing words and phrases. Compare your answers with a partner.

PART 1: Raw materials

Ms Roberts: OK. Are you all ready? Let's start our factory tour. Making paint begins with the raw materials. We use lots of
5 different powders, water, oils and other chemicals. They all arrive at the factory **(1)** … We store them here, in these big tanks. Every day, we use about **(2)** … kilograms of powder.

→ powder   → to store   → tank

PART 2: Production and quality control

Ms Roberts: OK. Let's go now to **(3)** ... part of the factory, the production area. This is the place where we make the paint. We make it in these big tanks. We do this all automatically. Can you see those people up there, with the **(4)** ... ? They're mixing the different powders and chemicals for the different paints. When the paint is ready, something very important happens. It's called Quality Control. Now, here we are. Oh, hi, Rachel. This is Rachel, everybody. She's a quality control technician. What are you doing at the moment, Rachel?

Rachel: Hi. I'm checking some paint. We don't want **(5)** ... with our products, so we check all the paints carefully before they go out of the factory.

PART 3: Warehouse and dispatch

Ms Roberts: OK, so we have the paint and we know that it's good quality. Now we put the paint into cans and we store it here, in the warehouse. **(6)** ... , we send the paint to shops or companies. We call this 'dispatch'. This big robot can load the paint quickly and easily onto lorries.

PART 4: Research and development and the offices

Ms Roberts: Just two more places now. Let's go here first. This is the laboratory. This is where we **(7)** ... new paints.
OK, and finally, here we are again in the offices. All the business and the administrative people work here – the people who **(8)** ... the raw materials, **(9)** ... the paints, look after the company's money and so on. So, that's it. I hope you enjoyed your quick tour!

D After the visit to Rolac Paints, Herr Wolf asked the apprentices some questions. Can you answer them? Give the answers in German.
→ More please! D – E

1 Welche Rohstoffe benutzt man bei der Herstellung von Farben?
2 Welche Rolle spielen Computer im Herstellungsprozess?
3 Welche Abteilung im Unternehmen ist für die Qualität der Produkte verantwortlich? Warum ist diese Abteilung so wichtig?
4 Wo werden a) die Produkte vor der Abfertigung gelagert und
b) neue Produkte entwickelt? Verwende bitte die englischen Begriffe.
5 Welche Rolle spielen die kaufmännischen Angestellten im Unternehmen? Bitte Beispiele nennen.

→ area → to mix → to put into → to load onto → administrative

4 More please!

A Adjectives and adverbs → Grammar 11

Which is right, a or b?

1. Jim is late for an appointment and he is driving his car very
   a) quick   b) *quickly*.
2. He doesn't usually drive like that. He normally drives quite
   a) slow   b) slowly.
3. Lots of doors in shops, factories and other places open and close
   a) automatic   b) automatically.
4. They are a) automatic   b) automatically doors.
5. The meeting starts at 9.00. Please be a) punctual   b) punctually.
6. This is a very a) good   b) well report, thanks.
7. You did this very a) good   b) well!
8. I think I speak English quite a) good   b) well, but I speak German better.
9. We lost the football match yesterday. Our team played
   a) bad   b) badly.
10. Don't go to that restaurant. The food is really a) bad   b) badly.

B Adjectives and adverbs → Grammar 11

Copy and fill in the table, then use the best words from the table (*adjective* or *adverb*) to finish the sentences below.

Adjective	Adverb
automatic	*automatically*
bad	*badly*
exact	?
good	?
punctual	?
quick	?
slow	?

1. Lots of processes in factories today happen *automatically* because of robots.
2. You speak English very ... !
3. The company's new products are very ... – everyone wants them.
4. I must buy a new computer. My old one is so ...
5. Sorry, I don't understand. Could you speak ..., please?
6. German trains usually arrive ... at the station.
7. Can you give me an ... description of the man?
8. The roads are covered in snow so don't drive ...
9. We played ... yesterday and lost the match.
10. Sarah woke up late this morning. She got up, had a ... shower, and ran out of the house.

C Greeting visitors

Two American businesspeople are just arriving at the offices of a factory in Germany – Mr Ramirez from the USA and his assistant. Stefanie Dabbert, the German factory manager's assistant, is meeting them. Do task 1 or 2 below.

Task 1

Choose the correct expressions to complete the dialogue. Write out the completed dialogue.

Stefanie	Mr Ramirez? Hello, **(1)** *I'm* Stefanie Dabbert, Herr Schenk's assistant.
Mr Ramirez	Hello, Ms Dabbert. **(2)** ...
Stefanie	**(3)** ... Kartex GmbH.
Mr Ramirez	Thanks. **(4)** ... . **(5)** ... my assistant, Megan Turner?
Stefanie	Nice to meet you, Ms Turner.
Ms Turner	**(6)** ..., Ms Dabbert. But please, **(7)** ... Megan.
Stefanie	Great, thanks. **(8)** ... Stefanie. OK, my boss's office is on the first floor. **(9)** ... .

And I'm
call me
Can I introduce
I'm
It's great to be here
Nice to meet you
Welcome to
Please come this way
Pleased to meet you too

Task 2

Complete the dialogue with the correct English words and phrases. Write out the full dialogue in English.

Stefanie	Mr Ramirez? Hello, **(1)** *ich heiße Stefanie Dabbert*. I'm Mr Schenk's assistant.
Mr Ramirez	Hello, Ms Dabbert. **(2)** *Freut mich, Sie kennen zu lernen*.
Stefanie	**(3)** *Willkommen bei Kartex GmbH*.
Mr Ramirez	**(4)** *Danke*. **(5)** *Es ist schön, hier zu sein*. **(6)** *Darf ich meine Assistentin Megan Turner vorstellen?*
Stefanie	**(7)** *Es freut mich, Sie kennen zu lernen, Frau Turner*.
Ms Turner	**(8)** *Bitte sagen Sie Megan zu mir*.
Stefanie	Great, thanks. **(9)** *Und ich bin Stefanie*. OK. **(10)** *Das Büro meines Chefs ist im ersten Stock. Bitte kommen Sie hier entlang*.

Check-in | Training | **More please!** | Check-out

D Company vocabulary

Match the English expressions with their German translations. All the words are about companies.

1	company	a	Abfertigung
2	factory	b	Büro
3	office	c	Büroarbeiter/in
4	cafeteria	d	erfinden
5	laboratory	e	Fabrik
6	to invent (a product)	f	herstellen
7	to make (a product)	g	Kantine
8	raw materials	h	Labor
9	warehouse	i	Lagerhalle
10	quality control	j	Qualitätsversicherung
11	dispatch	k	Roboter
12	robot	l	Rohstoffe
13	technician	m	Techinker/in
14	office worker	n	Unternehmen

E Company vocabulary

What are these people, places and things? All the words have to do with companies.

1 The place where you go first when you visit a company. A receptionist works here. *The reception desk.*
2 The part of the factory where the company manufactures its products.
3 A place in a factory where visitors and workers can get a meal or a cup of coffee.
4 A person who works in quality control.
5 Electronic machines which can design products and control processes and which you also use in offices to send emails.
6 The place in a factory where you store products before you dispatch them.
7 A person who buys your product.

F Key words

Find the correct words and phrases at the bottom of pages 27–31 and complete these sentences. Use the correct forms.

1 I always arrive ... for my lessons – I'm never late.
2 Sorry, my English isn't very good. Could you speak ... , please?
3 We have factories and offices around the world but our ... is in Munich in Germany.
4 If you want to paint your home, you can buy paint in a ... shop.
5 Can I ... my colleague Mr Simms?
6 The place where you go into a building is called the ...
7 We make our products then we ... them onto lorries and dispatch them.

5 Now you

A The apprentices have to write a report for Herr Wolf about their visit to Rolac. You're one of the apprentices. Write a report (about 100 words) in English. Include the following points.

1. What product(s) does the company make?
2. How does the company manufacture its product(s)? (Describe the main processes.)
3. Did you meet any of the workers at the company? What was their job?
4. What was the most interesting thing you saw / learned?

B **PROJECT** Find out about a company. It can be small or large, in the USA, Japan etc. or in your town. Make a poster.

So läuft's besser
Sehr viele Unternehmen haben Websites in mehreren Sprachen. Tipp: Vergleiche die englische und die deutsche Website eines Unternehmens. So kannst du leicht die wichtigsten Vokabeln lernen.

Video Lounge Plans

Jasmine, an English PA, is looking after two Australian businessmen, John Carter and Paul Rogers. She is explaining the schedule (the plans) for their visit to her company. Watch and put the plans in the right order.

a taxi to the airport
b visiting the test facility and meeting Jim Gibson (the test manager)
c Diane will show them some ideas for the new equipment (they want to buy)
d dinner with Diane and Mr Harris, the Managing Director of Jasmine's company
e meeting Chris Fox, the factory manager (with Jasmine's boss, Diane)

Unit 4
Global business

Check-in | Training | More please! | Check-out

1 Goods in a supermarket

R, P
A 2.10

A Read the short text below and answer the questions.

This delivery lorry is delivering goods to a British supermarket. The truck is delivering food, but supermarkets are often very big and they also sell other things like clothes, electronic goods and books. Lots of the things are made in Britain, perhaps even in the store. The bread in many supermarkets is made in a bakery in the store, for example. But lots of other things aren't from Britain. They are made in other countries around the world.

1 Describe the picture at the top opposite.
2 List some things you can often find in big British supermarkets. Where are they made?

R, P **B** Goods in supermarkets can come from around the world. Here are some things that you often find in supermarkets. Can you match them to the countries?

1 Camembert cheese
   I think this is made / produced in …
2 Pepperoni sausage
3 Hershey's chocolate
4 Electronics goods
   I think these are often made in …
5 Orange marmalade

Asia
Britain
France
Italy
The USA

P, I **C** Talk in class. Do you have things with you today which are made in another country? Where are those products made?

I have a … / a pair of … / some … (in class with me today.)
I think it / the … is made in …
I think they / the … are made in …
On the label, it say that it (they) is (are) made in …
I'm not sure where … is / are made (but I don't think it's in Germany / Europe).

→ to deliver   → goods   → store   → to be made / produced

Am Ende von Unit 4 kann ich:

— über internationale Unternehmen sprechen und schreiben,
— sagen, wo und wie Produkte hergestellt werden,
— etwas über die Vor- und Nachteile der Globalisierung sagen.

Unit 4 Global business 37

Check-in Training More please! Check-out

2 Thorben's new computer

R **A Read about Thorben. Why is he happy today? What did he do two weeks ago? What happened this morning?**

Thorben Stalke lives in Göttingen. Two weeks ago, he ordered a new computer online, and this morning the computer company delivered it to his flat. The new computer is brilliant – much better than his old one. And it wasn't too expensive. Now he can play games much more quickly and surf the Internet a lot more easily. Thorben is really happy.

R **B Thorben's computer is a typical desktop PC. But how does the company make its PCs? Look at the diagram on the next page and answer the questions below.**

1 Different parts of the computer are made in different countries. Where are the monitors made?
   They're made in …
2 What about the mice? Where are they made?
3 Another important part of a computer is the keyboard. Where are the keyboards manufactured?
4 The computer tower is the place where you find all the electronics – the hard drive, the motherboard and the CPU (central processing unit), for example. Where are the towers and all the things in them produced?
5 Before customers buy a computer, the company assembles all the different parts – it builds a computer. Where are the company's computers assembled?

P **C Now look at the diagram on the right. How was Thorben's new computer assembled? Finish the sentences.**

1 First, all the parts *were made* (make) around the world.
2 The parts **…** (transport) to Ireland.
3 Thorben's computer **…** (assemble).
4 Next, it **…** (transport) to Germany.
5 It **…** (store) in a warehouse.
6 Finally, the computer **…** (deliver) to his flat.

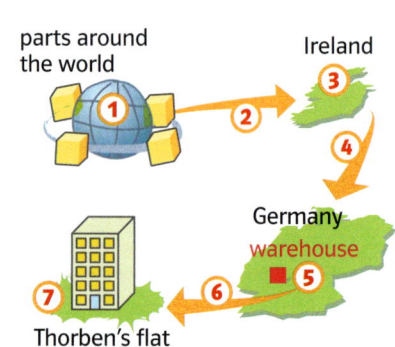

38 → to manufacture → to produce → to assemble → to transport

P **D** What are the missing forms?

Das Passiv		→ More please **A** – **C**
	simple present	simple past
the computer / it	? made	? produced
the monitors / they	? manufactured	? transported

Check-in | Training | More please! | Check-out

3 Is globalisation good or bad?

A 2.11

A Read the three texts below and on the next page. Two are *for* globalisation and one is *against*. Which are they?

Mary Makusa is from Kenya in East Africa. She has a small farm where she grows flowers. She's one of hundreds of small farmers in Kenya who are now flower growers. "The biggest industry in Kenya is growing tea," Mary
5 says. "But the second biggest is now growing flowers. It's more important than coffee or tourism." Mary's flowers aren't sold in Kenya. They're sold in supermarkets in Britain. They're transported to Britain by plane, and they're on sale in 24 hours. "Globalisation is good for me," says Mary. "I can sell my flowers on the world market."

Flowers in a British supermarket. Over 70% of the flowers are **imported from Kenya**.

Sunil Roy is from the city of Bangalore in southern India. Bangalore is an old and beautiful city, but in the 1980s and 90s lots of new buildings were built there. Today, it's India's most high-tech city – it's sometimes called the
5 'Silicon Valley of India'. Like thousands of other young people in Bangalore, Sunil works in a call centre. He's a computer technician, and every day he talks on a telephone helpline to people in Britain about their computer problems. Most of Sunil's friends also work in call centres for big banks and
10 other companies in Europe or the USA. "Globalisation is good for me," says Sunil. "We all speak English in India so the language isn't a problem. I earn a good salary and my life is much better than the life of my parents."

→ (to be) on sale   → the world market   → technician

Amjad lives 2300 kilometres from Sunil in a town in Pakistan. He's 10 years old but he doesn't go to school. He works every day in a small factory. He makes footballs. Amjad can make one football a day. For a football, he earns about one euro.
5 Amjad has to work. His family is very poor and they need his money. Around the world today, there are about 250 million – yes, 250 million! – children like Amjad. They work in factories, in mines, and lots work on farms. Big companies in Europe and the USA want to make their products very cheaply. The products (footballs,
10 clothes, trainers, carpets and many other things) are made by children in poor countries like Pakistan. Then they are sold in shops in Europe – where they're often expensive. Globalisation is good for big, global companies. But for Amjad it isn't so good.

R, P **B Finish the sentences with information from the three texts.**

1 Growing flowers is more important in Kenya than ...
2 Mary's flowers aren't sold in ... They're transported to supermarkets in ...
3 Globalisation is good for Mary because ...
4 The city of Bangalore changed in the 1980s and 90s when ...
5 Today, one name for the city is ...
6 Globalisation is good for Sunil because ...
7 Amjad can't go to school because ...
8 There are ... children like Amjad around the world today.
9 Globalisation is bad for Amjad but good for ...

P **C Is globalisation good or bad? Write a short text. Use the three stories as examples, and the useful phrases below.**

Globalisation is good for some people but bad for others ...

Useful phrases
on the one hand ... but on the other (hand) · one reason (why globalisation is good / bad) is that ... · another / a second / a third reason ... · for example, ... · from this we can see that ... · finally, we can say that ... · on the whole ...

P **D Give the German for *by*.**

Das Passiv mit *by*	→ More please **D – H**

Footballs are often made **by** children in poor countries.
These products were made **by** young girls in Pakistan.

→ (one) day   → to earn   → on the one hand   → on the other
→ on the whole

Hier und dort
Diese Beispiele der modernen, globalen Geschäftswelt zeigen, warum Englisch *die* Weltsprache geworden ist. Wenn beispielsweise Chinesen mit Deutschen Geschäfte machen, sprechen sie Englisch. Ohne eine gemeinsame Sprache könnten sie sich nicht verständigen. Außerdem ist Englisch für Millionen von Menschen weltweit die offizielle Amtssprache – wie für Mary aus Kenia und Sunil aus Indien.

Check-in | Training | **More please!** | Check-out

4 More please!

A The passive (simple present) → Grammar 10
**Complete the sentences with the verbs in brackets (...).
Use the *simple present passive*.**

1 Lots of products today *are made* (to make) in Asia.
2 This cheese **...** (to make) in France.
3 All the meat in our supermarkets **...** (to produce) on farms in Britain.
4 And all our bread **...** (to make) in bakeries in our stores.
5 First, the bicycles **...** (to manufacture) in our factory.
6 Then the bikes **...** (to store) in our warehouse.
7 Finally, they **...** (to deliver) to shops where people buy them.

B The passive (simple past) → Grammar 10
**Complete the sentences with the verbs in brackets (...).
Use the *simple past passive*.**

1 This old vase *was made* (to make) in China about 600 years ago.
2 I ordered the book online and it **...** (to deliver) yesterday.
3 The products **...** (to manufacture) in the USA and then they **...** (to transport) to Europe by sea.
4 Three million tonnes of chocolate **...** (to produce) worldwide last year.
5 It was a catastrophe. All our products **...** (to store) in a big warehouse and the warehouse burned down.

This is our best-selling T-shirt. It's made in China.

C The passive (simple present / simple past) → Grammar 10
**Complete the sentences with the verbs in brackets (...).
Use the *simple present passive* or the *simple past passive*.**

1 The products in a modern supermarket *are made* (to make) in many different countries.
2 10 billion litres of beer **...** (to produce) last year in Germany.
3 Our bread is fresh because it **...** (to make) daily here in our store.
4 I ordered the product online and it **...** (to delivered) the next day.
5 This is the last part of the manufacturing process in our factory. The cars **...** (to assemble) here.
6 Normally, our goods **...** (to transport) by sea but sometimes, when it is urgent, we send them by air.
7 It is amazing to think that this beautiful jewellery **...** (to make) over 1,000 years ago.
8 The raw materials for our products **...** (to store) in this warehouse.

D Passive sentences with *by* → Grammar 10

Look at the diagram, then write the *active* sentences below again as *passive* sentences with *by*.

1. A Chinese company makes our T-shirts.
   Our T-shirts …
2. Lots of young people play computer games.
3. A German company manufactures these cars.
4. A logistics company delivers our products.
5. Farmers in France produce this cheese.

active sentence		
Amjad	made	this football.
passive sentence		
This football	was made by	Amjad.

E Passive sentences with *by* (irregular verbs) → Grammar 10

Copy the table below and write in the past participles (3rd Form) of these irregular verbs. Then write the *active* sentences below again as *passive* sentences with *by*.

verb	past participle	verb	past participle
to build	*built*	to grow	*grown*
to buy	?	to speak	?
to eat	?	to write	?

1. A farmer in Kenya grew these flowers.
   These flowers were grown by a farmer in Kenya.
2. My dog ate my homework.
3. The Beatles wrote this song.
4. Millions of people speak English.
5. Some students built this model plane.
6. A friend bought my old car.

F Passive sentences with *by* → Grammar 10

Write the *active* sentences below again as *passive sentences* with *by*.

1. Farmers in Spain grow these oranges.
   These oranges are grown by farmers in Spain.
2. A company in Taiwan makes our motherboards.
3. A German company built this call centre.
4. Unfortunately, children in poor countries make many everyday products.
5. Did you know? A French architect built the Statue of Liberty in New York.
6. A logistics company transports our products.
7. Customers around the world buy our famous German sausages.
8. Millions of people in India speak English as their second language.

The Statue of Liberty **was given** to the American people by France when America became independent after a war with the British.

Check-in | Training | **More please!** | **Check-out**

P ▲ **G Active and passive sentences** → Grammar 10

In the pairs of sentences below, one sentence is *active* and the other is *passive*. Which is which? Use the verb in brackets (...) to complete both sentences.

1 (to make)
   a We *make* these products in our factory.
   b These products *are made* in our factory.
2 (to transport)
   a In our modern, globalised world, goods ... around the world.
   b The company ... its products around the world.
3 (to manufacture)
   a The trainers ... in Asia and then they are sold in Europe.
   b An Asian firm ... the trainers and sells them in Europe.
4 (to write)
   a My favourite band ... this song.
   b This song ... by my favourite band.
5 (to open)
   a A famous film star ... the new store.
   b The store ... by a famous film star.

P ▲ **H Active and passive sentences** → Grammar 10

Complete the text with the verbs in brackets. Be careful! Some sentences are *active*, some are *passive*.

In our modern, globalised world, goods **(1)** *are manufactured* (to manufacture) around the world. Then they **(2)** ... (to transport) often thousands of miles and we **(3)** ... (to buy) them in our shops.

For people in many countries, globalisation is a good thing. Countries like India and China now **(4)** ... (to make) lots of the products which we **(5)** ... (to use) in Europe, and as a consequence, people in those countries are richer. Unfortunately, however, some of those products **(6)** ... (to make) by poor children and others who **(7)** ... (to work) in terrible conditions and who **(8)** ... (to earn) almost no money for their work.

There is another problem with globalisation, too. When we **(9)** ... (to transport) goods around the world, it is not good for the environment. Until around 50 years ago, most products in our shops **(10)** ... (to produce) locally, so they did not need to travel far. Some people **(11)** ... (to think) that we should not buy goods from abroad – especially fresh fruit and vegetables, for example. Products like these which **(12)** ... (to grow) locally are much better.

R, P ▲ **I Key words**

Find the key words and phrases from pages 37–40 below. Choose three and write a sentence with each.

GOODSLORRYONTHEONEHANDSAUSAGESTORETOASSEMBL
ETOEARNTOBEONSALETOTRANSPORTWORLDMARKET

44

5 Now you

I, P **A Make a survey in your class then write about the results.**

1. How many of the things which you have in class (or at home) were made in Germany? How many were made in another country? Where? Find out about as many things as you can.
2. In class, make a survey and a graph. Then write about the results:
   About 80% of our clothes / jeans / trainers were made in another country.
   Only about 20% of our clothes were made in Germany.
   Over 90% of all our electronic goods were made in another country / overseas.

= made in Germany

P **B PROJECT Make a poster. Choose *one* of the ideas below.**

1. Find out how something is made and make a poster. Even simple, everyday things like toothpaste are often very complicated! Use pictures and words and show a diagram of the process.
2. FAIRTRADE is an idea to help workers like Amjad in Pakistan and other poor people around the world. Find out more about it on the internet and make a poster.

Video Lounge How was your visit?

Yesterday, Mr Carter and Mr Rogers visited Jasmine's company's test facility. Jasmine is asking them about their visit. Watch and say if the sentences below are true (T) or false (F). Then watch again and correct the false sentences.

1. John (the older man) thought the visit was very interesting.
2. The two men saw the computer centre.
3. Jasmine tells Mr Rogers how much the computer centre cost.
4. Paul didn't see the testing equipment for the pumps.
5. The two men stayed at the facility for a couple (= two) hours.
6. After the visit, Jasmine's boss Diane met the two men and took them to dinner.
7. John doesn't like Italian food very much.

Unit 5
A month in New Zealand

✚ Check-in | Training | More please! | Check-out

1 In Christchurch

R, P
A 2.12

A Read about Sven and Daniela and answer the questions.

Sven Heiderich and Daniela Stollenwerk are from Germany. They are apprentices with a big German car manufacturer. They are in the marketing department. They usually work in Germany, of course. But their company has offices around the world, and this month they are in Christchurch, on the South Island of New Zealand. It is a brilliant opportunity for them to see a new country and to practise their English.

1 What do you learn about Christchurch from the text?
2 Describe the two pictures – who and what can you see? What are Sven and Daniela doing?

P
B Daniela and Sven arrived in New Zealand on 1 January. It's now two weeks later, 15 January. Look at the diagram below and the Tips and tricks box and finish the sentences.

Tips and tricks

Since *1 Jan* = Zeitpunkt
For *two weeks* = Zeitraum

Vorsicht! Auf Deutsch heißen *since* und *for* beide 'seit'!

Daniela and Sven have been in New Zealand … two weeks.
They … been there … 1 January.

P, I
C Make some sentences about yourself and tell the class.

I have been a student at this college since …
I have lived in my hometown for …
I have … for / since …

Am Ende von Unit 5 kann ich: ✚

— über Neuseeland reden und schreiben,
— sagen, seit wann etwas schon andauert,
— wichtige Redewendungen im Alltag richtig benutzen.

→ manufacturer   → (marketing) department   → for / since

Unit 5 A month in New Zealand   **47**

Check-in | Training | More please! | Check-out

2 The land of the Kiwis

A Before Daniela and Sven went to New Zealand, they read about the country online. Read the web page and find the best headings A – F for the paragraphs 1 – 6 in the text.

A Small, beautiful and famous
B Do you speak Kiwi?
C Sport
D People
E The land of the Kiwis
F Cities

(1) …
Yes, kiwis are a kind of fruit. In fact, lots of the kiwis that we eat come from New Zealand. But a kiwi is also a kind of bird
5 and it lives only in New Zealand. New Zealanders use the name of the bird for themselves – as a nickname. They say: "I'm a Kiwi. I'm from New Zealand."

(2) …
10 White people have lived in New Zealand for around 250 years. The islands were discovered in 1768 by the English explorer Captain Cook, and many British people came there after him, which is why English is spoken in New Zealand. But the first people in New Zealand were the Maoris (who built these famous statues). Maori
15 people have lived in New Zealand for 1,000 years and today they are about 15 per cent of the population of the country.

(3) …
New Zealand isn't a big country. It is a little smaller than Germany. But it is extremely beautiful with mountains and lakes. Since 2000
20 it has also been famous on screen. The film director Peter Jackson filmed the *Lord of the Rings* films there, so when you watch the *LOTR* movies, you can see many places in New Zealand.

(4) …
New Zealanders love sports. There's swimming, skiing, surfing,
25 canoeing, mountain climbing, bungee jumping and lots more. One of the most popular sports is rugby. Before a match, the New Zealand rugby team always does a Maori war dance called a 'haka'. Look online for the dance – it's very dramatic!

→ nickname   → to discover sth   → explorer   → (film) director
→ bungee jumping

48

(5) ...
30 New Zealand doesn't have many big cities. The biggest is Auckland on the North Island with a population of 1.3 million (about a quarter of all the people in New Zealand). It isn't the capital, however. That is Wellington, also on the North Island (population 450,000).

35 (6) ...
When New Zealanders speak English, they have a Kiwi accent. It is almost the same as the accent of people from Australia. They have some Kiwi words and phrases, too. *Hello* is *G'day (Good day)* as in Australia. On the beach, people often wear *jandals*, that's *flip-flops* in
40 British English. And, of course, everyone loves a *barbie*, a barbecue in the summer (December – March!).

Wellington • Auckland
North Island
Wellington •
• Christchurch
South Island

R, P **B True or false? Correct the false sentences.**

1 New Zealanders call themselves Kiwis because that fruit comes from New Zealand.
2 The first inhabitants of New Zealand were the Maoris.
3 New Zealand is a little bigger than Germany.
4 A 'haka' is a sport that New Zealanders love.
5 The capital of New Zealand isn't the biggest city.
6 New Zealanders and Australians have a different accent to British people when they speak English.

P **C Finish the *How long ...?* sentences about New Zealand.**

	Then	Now	How long ...?
1	Maoris came to New Zealand 1,000 years ago.	Maoris live in New Zealand now.	Maoris *have lived* in New Zealand ... 1,000 years.
2	The first white people came to New Zealand in the 18th century.	White people live in New Zealand today.	They ... in New Zealand ... the 18th century.
3	New Zealand became famous on screen in 2000.	The country is famous on screen today.	It ... famous on screen ... 2000.

P **D What are the missing forms?**

The present perfect with *for / since*				→ More please! A – C	
I	have			since	2010.
he / she / it	?	lived here		?	5 years.
we / you / they	?				

→ population   → capital   → accent   → inhabitant

Unit 5 A month in New Zealand   49

Check-in — **Training** — More please! — Check-out

3 Be polite, please.

P **A** Sven and Daniela have to speak English every day in New Zealand – at work and with the family where they are staying, the MacKenzies. Look at the three pictures below. Where do you think they are? What are they doing?

A 2.14 **B** You will hear three conversations. Listen and match the conversations (1–3) and the pictures (A–C).

P, R **C** What are the missing phrases in the three conversations? Note down your answers, then listen again and check.

1
Mrs MacKenzie	(1) ... some more pancakes, Daniela?
Daniela	Yes, please, Mrs MacKenzie. They're delicious.
Mrs MacKenzie	Here you are.
Daniela	(2) ...
Mrs MacKenzie	Sven? What about you?
Sven	They're fantastic, but I'm afraid I'm absolutely full up!
Mr MacKenzie	What about some orange juice?
Sven	Mmm, yes, please. (3) ...

2
Daniela	Excuse me, Mrs MacKenzie. (4) ...
Mrs MacKenzie	Sure. What's the problem, Daniela?
Daniela	Well, it's really hot in the day but it's cold at night. (5) ... another blanket for my bed, please?
Mrs MacKenzie	(6) ... Come on. Let's get one now.

→ pancake(s) → blanket → absolutely (full up) → Let's ...

3

Ben	G'day, guys. How are you this morning?
Sven	G'day, Ben. We're fine, thanks.
Ben	Hey, listen. Some of us are going to go to the beach after work tomorrow. **(7)** … to come?
Daniela	Yeah, cool. Thanks.
Ben	Do you have togs?
Sven	**(8)** …
Ben	Do you have *togs*?
Sven	Sorry, I don't understand. **(9)** … 'togs' mean?
Ben	Sorry, yeah, it's a Kiwi word. It means, you know, a swimsuit.
Daniela	Oh, right. **(10)** … Yes, I have togs.
Sven	Me too.
Ben	Great. See you then.

P, I **D** Work in small groups. Practise the conversations.

R **E** Match the phrases 1 – 5 with a correct answer A – G. There's sometimes more than one answer.

1 Would you like …?
2 Here you are.
3 Could you help me, please?
4 Could I …?
5 What does … mean?

a It means, you know, …
b Of course.
c Thank you.
d Yes, please. That would be nice.
e Cool! Thanks.
f Sure. What's the problem?
g I'm afraid I'm absolutely full up!

Would you …?

Could I …?

P, I **F** Now YOU. Work in your groups again. Write another conversation, then read it to the class. Use the phrases on these two pages. Below are some ideas. → More please! D – G

breakfast / lunch / dinner
toast · coffee · milk · soup · bread · dessert · potatoes

Could you help me, please?
· phone your parents
· have a shower
· borrow some 'jandals'
· go to the beach / cinema with some friends

Pardon?
· "Did you see the rugby match on TV yesterday? What did you think of the Haka?"
· "Kiwis are flightless birds."

Hier und dort
Wenn Deutsche Englisch sprechen, wird es von Muttersprachlern oft als sehr direkt und vielleicht etwas unhöflich empfunden. Um diesen Eindruck zu vermeiden, verwende so oft wie möglich die Ausdrücke *Would you like …? Could I …? Please …* usw.

→ to mean   → See you.   → to borrow

4 More please!

A The present perfect with *for/since* → Grammar 4
Complete the sentences with *since* or *for*.

1 Maoris have lived in New Zealand *for* 1,000 years but white people have lived there only .... around 1770.
2 I have lived in my hometown .... 16 years.
3 How long have you had your laptop?
   – .... last Friday!
4 How long have you been a student at this college?
   – I have been here .... a year and a half.
5 We are the Richardson family. We came to New Zealand from Britain and we have lived here now .... three years.

B The present perfect with *for/since* → Grammar 4
Make sentences.

1 I / live / here / two years
   I have lived here for two years.
2 They / be / at college / 8 o'clock this morning
3 I / know / my best friend / 2009
4 Matt / work / in New York / the last six months
5 We / have / this computer / about three years
6 Nicole / be / in our class / January
7 I / learn / English / I was 10 years old

C The present perfect with *for/since* → Grammar 4
In the groups of sentences below, one verb is in the *simple present*, one in the *simple past* and one in the *present perfect*. Complete the sentences with the correct forms.

1 a My family *moved* (to move) to New Zealand last year.
   b We .... (to live) in New Zealand now.
   c We .... (to live) here since last year.

2 a Saskia .... (to work) in England for the last three months.
   b She .... (to go) to England three months ago.
   c She .... (to be) in England now.

3 a I .... (to learn) English at college.
   b I .... (to start) learning English when I was 10 years old.
   c I .... (to learn) English for around seven years.

4 a We .... (to buy) our computer in 2013.
   b We .... (to have) our computer since 2013.
   c We .... (to use) the computer every day.

P △ **D Polite expressions**

You are staying in England at the moment with the Smith family – Mrs Smith, Mr Smith, their daughter Catherine and their son Mike. Finish the conversations below with the best phrases.

1 **Mrs Smith** Do you like this roast beef? We often have it on Sundays.
  You Yes, it's *delicious*!

2 **Mrs Smith** Would you like some more pudding?
  You Oh, no ... , Mrs Smith. I'm ... .

3 **You** Hi, Mike. ... ?
  Mike Sure, if I can. What do you want to know?

4 **You** ... , Mr Smith. Are you busy?
  Mr Smith No, not at all. How can I help?
  You Well, there's a football match on TV this evening between Germany and Spain. ... watch it, please?
  Mr Smith Of course. I'll watch it with you!

5 **Catherine** I'm going to town this afternoon. Would you like to come with me?
  You ... ...

could I ...?
could you help me, please?
excuse me
full up
thanks
that would be great
yes, please
delicious

M ▲ **E Polite expressions (mediation)**

Will, a New Zealand teenager, is staying with you in Germany at the moment. Your parents don't speak English so they ask you to be their interpeter. Give the English phrases.

Your parents ask …
1 ob Will mehr Kartoffelsalat haben möchte.
  Would you like some more potato salad?
2 ob er mit uns in die Stadt fahren möchte.
3 ob er seine Eltern anrufen möchte.
4 Will möchte uns um etwas bitten, aber wir verstehen nicht, worum es geht. Wie können wir ihm helfen?
5 Will hat mich gestern um ein zweites Kopfkissen *(pillow)* gebeten. Hier ist es, bitte schön.
6 ob Will jetzt satt ist.

Check-in | Training | **More please!** | Check-out

F Saying you don't understand

When you are in another country there are often things you don't understand. Dirk is in the States at the moment. Right now he's talking to Luke, a high school student. Write their conversation again in the right order.

Luke **Dirk**
Airhead.
    Great, thanks. And you?
It means, you know, idiot.
    Sorry, I don't understand. What does 'airhead' mean?
Hey, Dirk. How's it going?
    Oh right. I understand now.
    Pardon?
Not so good. I have loads of homework this evening.
My math teacher Mr Roth is a real airhead.

Luke Hey, Dirk. How's it going?
Dirk …

G Saying you don't understand

An English-speaking friend is in Germany with you. She speaks a little German but doesn't understand the expressions below. Can you explain in English? Choose three and write a short explanation. Use your dictionary if necessary and the useful phrases below.

1 eine '3' (Note)
2 Du spinnst!
3 Geisterfahrer
4 eine Fahrkarte abstempeln
5 Wurstbude
6 ferngucken

It means (that) …
It's a person who … / a place where
You have to do this when you …
In Germany, when we do a test we get a grade from … to …
very good / good / satisfactory (average) /
sufficient / poor / unsatisfactory (you fail)

H Key words

Find the correct words and phrases at the bottom of pages 47–51 and complete these sentences. Use the correct forms.

1 'Marketingabteilung' means … in English.
2 Captain Cook was a famous … He … Australia and New Zealand.
3 The … of Germany is around 82 million. That means it has 82 million … .
4 You speak English really well – you have almost no German … .
5 I can't eat another thing. I'm absolutely … .
6 Can I … your dictionary, please?
  – Sure, but don't forget to give it back!

5 Now you

P **A** You have a friend in New Zealand who wants to know about Germany and where you live. Look at the map and the FAST FACTS box and write a short text (100–150 words). There are some phrases below to help you.

Hi … (name of your friend)
You wanted to know about Germany.
I live in … (town / city) *which is in the north / south / …*
I have lived here for … years / since … / all my life
My hometown is big / small / has a population of …
My country has a population of …
It has been one country … 1989. Before that it was divided into West and East Germany.
New Zealand has lots of mountains and lakes. Germany is …
In Germany we speak … but we all learn English at school.
In Germany people like (sports / food / entertainment). *My favourite … is …*

GERMANY	Fast Facts
Population	82,490,000
Capital	Berlin, 3,327,000
Language	German
Currency	Euro
History	1 country since 1989
Geography	Flat in north, mountains in south

Video Lounge Goodbye

It's the last day of Mr Rogers's and Mr Carter's visit. Jasmine is saying goodbye.

R, P **A** Watch the video.

1 How are the men travelling to the airport?
2 How long is the journey normally from the office to the airport?
3 Why can the journey be different on Fridays?
4 What is the last thing Jasmine says at the end?

M **B** Watch again and find the English for:

Es war schön, dich / Sie wiederzusehen.
Ich bin froh, dass es dir / Ihnen gefallen hat (= dein / Ihr Besuch).
Bis bald, hoffe ich.
Tschüs. Pass auf dich auf!

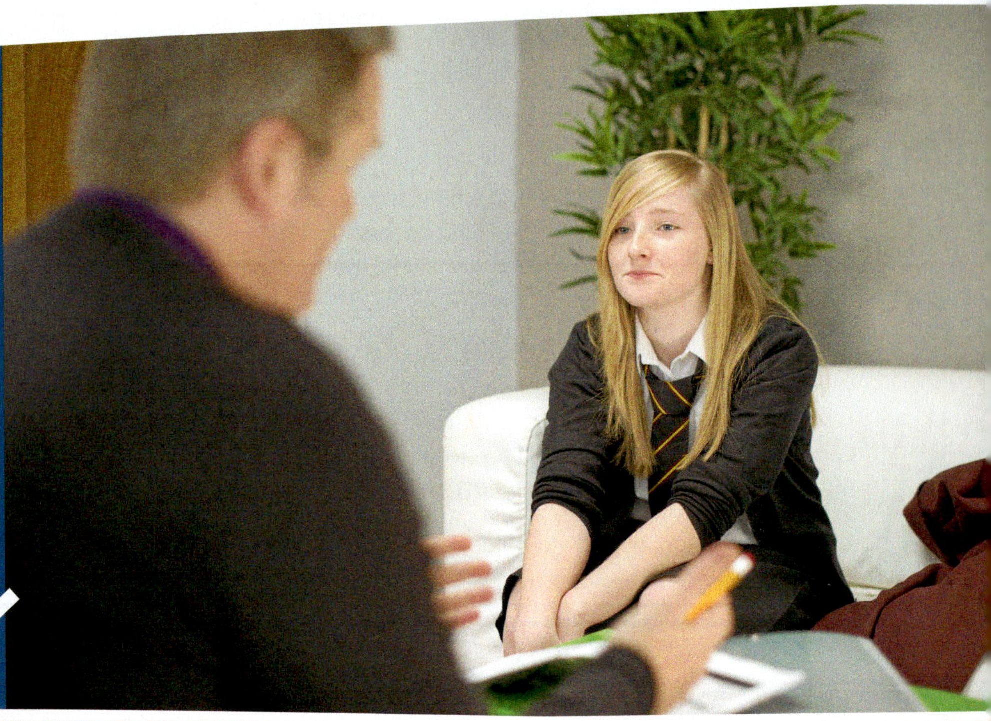

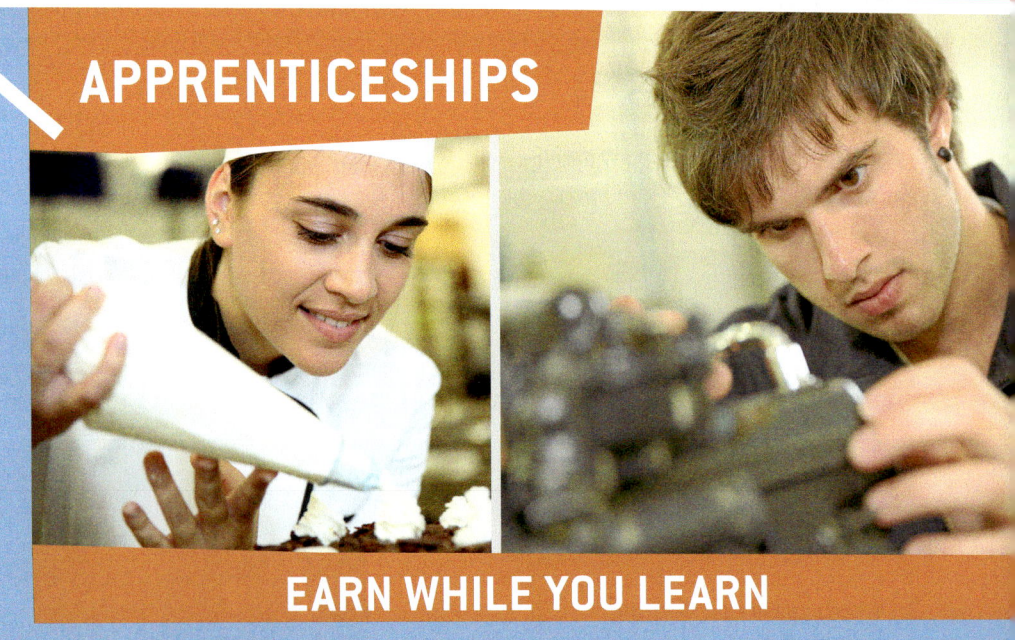

APPRENTICESHIPS

EARN WHILE YOU LEARN

Unit 6
Apprenticeships

a4d4sj

Check-in | Training | More please! | Check-out

1 Earn while you learn

R, P
A 2.15

A Read about Lara and answer the questions.

The girl in the picture opposite is Lara Summers. She lives in England and she's 16 years old. At the end of this school year, Lara will take her GCSE exams – those are the exams that pupils take at 16 in all the basic subjects like English and maths. But Lara isn't sure what she would like to do after that. Today, she's talking to one of the teachers at her school, Mr Anderson, who gives the pupils advice about careers.

1 What do you learn in the text about education in England?
2 Describe the picture in detail – who? where? what? why?

R, P

B Mr Anderson listened to Lara and made some notes, then he gave her some advice. Look at the Tips and tricks box and finish what he said below.

- doesn't want to stay at school
- wants a 'good job' with a qualification
- loves make-up and beauty
- would like to earn money straight away

"OK, Lara. You want to leave school and to earn money straight away. But you also want a a good job, so you need some training. Well, what about an apprenticeship? There are lots of good jobs in the beauty industry. If you *did* (do) an apprenticeship, you ___ (get) a qualification and you ___ (earn) money, too. Earn while you learn!"

Tips and tricks
If-sentences type 2
If Lara **stayed** at school, she **would be** unhappy.

IF + simple past / would

Am Ende von Unit 6 kann ich:
— über Lehrstellen sprechen und schreiben,
— an einem Vorstellungsgespräch teilnehmen,
— sagen, was passieren würde, wenn ...

→ GCSE (General Certificate of Secondary Education)
→ to take an exam   → (to give sb.) advice   → straight away
→ to do an apprenticeship

Unit 6 Apprenticeships   57

Check-in ✚ **Training** | More please! | Check-out

2 If you did an apprenticeship in England, …

A 2.16

Imagine that you did an apprenticeship in England. The text below is from a UK government brochure about apprenticeships. Read it and do the tasks on the next page.

APPRENTICESHIPS: earn while you learn

What are apprenticeships?
Anyone who is 16 or older can do an apprenticeship. Apprenticeships last between one and four years. Apprentices work alongside experienced tradespeople to learn the skills they need for their
5 job and while they learn, they earn a basic wage. They also study, usually one day a week at a vocational college, and at the end of their training they get a qualification. A typical apprentice works a minimum of 30 hours per week. Because apprentices are employees, they get paid holidays (a minumum of 20 days per year plus national
10 holidays).

Why do an apprenticeship?
Doing an apprenticeship means that you:
· earn money while you learn
· get paid holidays
15 · get good practical training
· get real qualifications.
Research also shows that people who begin their career with an apprenticeship earn more in their lifetime than a person without training.

20 **Types of apprenticeships**
There are apprenticeships in many different industries and you can be an apprentice with a large, national company or a small local one. At the moment, there are 1,400 different jobs in England where it is possible to do an apprenticeship. The apprenticeship you choose
25 depends on your interests, your ability, and the opportunities in your part of the country.

How do I find an apprenticeship?
There is a national database in England for
30 apprenticeships. Go to our apprenticeship website and register your name. You can then find, read about, and apply for apprenticeships directly.

Hands-on learning.
Apprentices work alongside experienced tradespeople to learn practical job skills.

There are **hundreds of different industries** in which you can do an apprenticeship from beauty therapy to building, and nursing to agriculture.

→ experienced → tradesperson / people → skill(s) → local (company) → to apply for sth.

R, P **A** **True or false? Correct the false sentences.**

1 If you did an apprenticeship in England, it would normally last five years.
2 You wouldn't earn any money.
3 You would normally spend one day a week at college.
4 You would get at least 20 days a year holiday and you would be paid while you were on holiday.
5 If you did an English apprenticeship, you would work for one of the country's largest companies.
6 If you wanted an apprenticeship, you would normally write to some companies in your part of the country.

R **B** **Here are some definitions. What word(s) do they define? All the words were in the text.**

1 A person who does an apprenticeship. *an apprentice*
2 A certificate etc. which shows that you finished your training successfully.
3 The days in the year when you don't have to work or study.
4 Another word for 'firm'.
5 The things you are interested in are your ….
6 Information which is stored on a computer.

P **C** **What do you know about jobs? Look at these jobs. How many sentences can you make? Use your dictionary if necessary.**

- Where would you work?
- What would you do in your job?
- What sort of people would you meet?
- What places (countries etc.) would you perhaps travel to?

If I were a … If I worked as a …, I would …

make-up artist   travel tour guide   computer games developer

P **D** **What are the missing forms?**

If-sentences Type 2   → More please **A - D**

If you …?… (be) a travel guide, you …?… (meet) lots of tourists.
You …?…(need) English if you …?… (work) for this company.

→ to be paid   → to last (5 years)   → (what) sort of (?)   → to need (English)

Check-in ✛ **Training** | More please! | Check-out

3 An interview

R, P **A** Meryem Gulec is from Bremen and after college she would like to become a flight attendant. Last week she saw this advertisement in a magazine. She wrote her CV and sent it to Mr Werner. Look at the CV now and answer the questions below. → More please! D

> AIR DEUTSCHLAND currently has a number of TRAINEESHIPS for flight attendants, check-in clerks, computer technicians and sales people. For further information, please contact Heiko Werner, Personnel Manager, on

1 Where in Bremen does Meryem live?
2 Where did she go to primary school?
3 When did she start and finish secondary school?
4 What qualification did she get at the end of secondary school?
5 Where does she go to college and what qualification does she want to get there?
6 Does Meryem have a part-time job? What does she do?
7 What computer programs can she use?
8 How well does she speak Turkish? And English?
9 What does she like doing in her free time?

CURRICULUM VITAE

Personal details
Name: Meryem Gulec
Address: Findorffstraße 20
                 28215 Bremen
Date of birth: 1998

Education and qualifications
Primary school: 2003-2007   Grundschule Burgdamm, Bremen
Secondary school: 2007-2013   Schulzentrum Findorff, Bremen
                                Qualification: Fachoberschulreife
College: 2013-   Berufskolleg Findorff
                                Studying for qualification as Kauffrau für
                                Touristik und Freizeit (=Management Assistant
                                for Tourism and Leisure)
Work experience: 2014-   Part-time job at Hapag-Lloyd Travel Agents, Bremen

Computer skills: Microsoft Word and Excel, social media
Languages: German (fluent), Turkish (mother tongue), English (good)
Interests: Travel, making clothes, singing

→ flight attendant   → CV (Curriculum Vitae)   → to contact sb.   → traineeship   → work experience

 B It's one month later, and Meryem is having a job interview at Air Deutschland with Mr Werner. You'll hear three parts of the interview. Listen and answer the questions.

A 2.17

PART 1 First, Mr Werner asks Meryem some questions about her CV. Listen and choose the correct answer a, b or c.

1 Meryem loves
  a going to airports.
  b flying.
  c staying in hotels.

2 Two years ago she flew to
  a London.
  b the USA.
  c Turkey.

3 Meryem sings in
  a a club for young people.
  b a rock band.
  c her bathroom at home.

PART 2 Mr Werner is talking to Meryem now about the work of a flight attendant. Listen and finish the sentences.

1 Meryem thinks that she would be a good flight attendant because
  – she loves travel and …
  – she also likes …
  – she also likes being …
2 If Meryem worked for Air Deutschland, she would only be at home …

PART 3 Listen to the end of Meryem's interview with Mr Werner. True or false? Note down T or F.

1 If Meryem got the traineeship, her training would last six months.
2 She would be in Bremen the first month.
3 After that, she would fly on normal flights but she wouldn't work as a flight attendant.
4 Mr Werner will contact Meryem tomorrow about the traineeship.

C Talk in class. What do YOU think? Did Meryem give good answers in her interview? Why (not)? Do you think that she will get the traineeship? → More please! E

Unit 6 Apprenticeships   **61**

4 More please!

A *If*-sentences type 2 → Grammar 9

Match the sentence halves.

1 If I had lots of money, — a he would get better marks at school.
2 If I lived in England, b you would perhaps meet Marie.
3 If you were a nurse, c I would speak English every day.
4 If you were an IT expert, d I would travel round the world.
5 If you came to my party, e they would give us our money back.
6 If Josh worked harder, f you would repair computers.
7 If we wrote to the company, g you would work in a hospital.

B *If*-sentences type 2 → Grammar 9

Complete the sentences with the correct forms of the verbs in brackets (. . .). Remember: *if*-sentences can begin with the *if*-part or the main clause (Hauptsatz)!

1 If I *had* (have) a job, I ... (earn) money.
2 I ... (earn) money if I ... (have) a job.
3 If you ... (work) as a tour guide, you ... (travel) a lot.
4 You ... (travel) a lot if you ... (be) a tour guide.
5 If she ... (do) an apprenticeship, she ... (learn) about a job from experienced tradespeople.
6 She ... (earn) money, too, if she ... (do) an apprenticeship.
7 Paul hates school. He ... (be) very unhappy if he ... (stay) here.
8 But if Christine ... (stay) at school, she ... (love) it.

C *If*-sentences type 2 → Grammar 9

Look at the pictures below and answer the questions on the next page with whole sentences.

1 Where (in what city) would you be if you saw the Eiffel Tower?
  I would be in … if I … .
2 If you saw the Brandenburg Gate, where would you be?
3 What would you eat if you went to the restaurant in picture 3?
4 What *wouldn't* you do if you saw the sign in picture 4?
5 What would you be if you had the job of the person in picture 5?

R, P ▲ **D** *If*-sentences type 2 → Grammar 9
A good way to spend time in an English-speaking country is to become an au pair. But what do you know about au pairs? Read the brochure below and answer the questions with whole sentences. Use *if*-sentences type 2.

Being an au pair is a great way to travel, learn about another country, and improve your English. We have au pair jobs in England and the USA. In the past, au pairs were always women, but today there are au pair jobs for men too.

What are the requirements?
To be an au pair you must:
· be aged between 17 and 27 (18 and 27 in the USA)
· be single (not married)
5 · have a passport in your country
· like children and want to learn about another country
· be ready to live for a minimum of 6 months in another country.
What do au pairs do?
Au pairs work a maximum of 25 hours a week. During this time, they
10 look after children and do light housework such as cleaning.
How much do au pairs earn?
For the work they do, au pairs earn on average €80 a month. They also live free with their host family – they get a room in the family's house and eat with the family. Au pairs pay their own travel costs from their
15 country to Britain or the USA.
What do au pairs do in their free time?
Most au pairs take the chance to go to a language school while they are in the country. They sometimes meet other au pairs in their town, too – we give you the addresses of other au pairs. Almost all au pairs
20 also travel around the country to see other regions and to visit interesting places.

1 Where would you live if you were an au pair?
  If you were an au pair, you …
2 How much would you earn if you had an au pair job?
3 Would you meet other au pairs if you worked as an au pair?
4 What work would you have to do if you were an au pair?
5 If you had an au pair job, what sorts of things would you be able to (could you) do in your free time?

Tips and tricks
Die *would*-Form von *can* ist entweder *would be able to* oder *could*.

Check-in | Training | **More please!** | Check-out

CURRICULUM VITAE

Personal details
Name: Andrew Michael West
Address: 23 Grove Park Avenue
Danbury DB3 4NR
Date of birth: 1997

Education and qualifications
Primary school: 2003–2008 Danbury Primary School
Secondary school: 2008–2013 Danbury Comprehensive
Qualifications: GCSEs in English, maths, history, French, science, IT
College: 2013– Danbury FE College
Studying for a qualification in IT

Work experience 2010–2011 Worked 12 months part-time at Freshco Supermarket, Danbury
2012 Work placement at Danbury Software Ltd. (3 weeks)

Skills: Computer programming, French (average)
Interests: Snowboarding, canoeing, football, computer gaming

R, P **E Talking about a CV** → Skills 7

▲ **Above you can see the CV of a young British student. Make and answer questions about it. Use the *simple past*.**

1 when / Andy / born?
   When was Andy born? He was born in 1997
2 where / go / to primary school?
3 where / go / to secondary school?
4 what / GCSEs / get / at secondary school?
5 when / start college?
6 where / work / in 2010 to 2011?
7 when / do / work placement / at Danbury Software Ltd.?

P **F Key words**

▲ **Find the correct words and phrases at the bottom of pages 57–60 and complete these sentences. Use the correct forms.**

1 I ... my GCSE exams last year.
2 I don't know what to do. Can you give me some ... , please?
3 He has been a mechanic for 20 years, so he is very ... .
4 The company is in my hometown. It's a ... company.
5 How long ... apprenticeships in England ... ?
   – Between one and four years.
6 What ... car do you have? – An old VW Beetle.
7 You can ... me on this number.
8 The people who bring you food and drinks on an aeroplane are called ... .

5 Now you

P, I **A** Write your CV in English. Look at Meryem's CV on page 60 for ideas. You can organise a gallery walk in class afterwards. If possible, use a computer and print out your CV. Think carefully about layout and headings. → Skills 5

P, I **B** Write about 100 words about the cartoon below. Compare your answer with a partner then report to the class.

- Who are the people?
- What is happening?
- What do you think? What would an interviewer say if someone did this?

Video Lounge Applying for a job

R, P **Maya decided last week that she would like to do a work placement in a hotel in Germany. Now she is having an interview with the hotel manager, Mr McFarlane – and he is a little scary! Watch the episode and answer the questions.**

1 What must Maya send Mr McFarlane before her interview?
2 Why does Maya want to work in a hotel?
3 And why in Germany?
4 What must you 'always remember' when you work in a hotel?
5 What would Maya like to do in the next five years?
6 What mistake does Maya make near the end of the interview?
7 Where (in what city) will she work?

Unit 7
Starting work

Check-in | Training | More please! | Check-out

1 This is me at work!

A Read about Connor and Brandon and answer the questions.

After years at school, Connor (top) and Brandon, two English teenagers, are finally at work. They both have apprenticeships, Connor as an industrial electrician and Brandon as an administrative assistant in an office. Both apprenticeships will last three years. Do the two young men like being apprentices? This is what they said:

Connor: I decided to do an apprenticeship in my last year at school and I really like working. For me, learning 'on the job' is brilliant.
Brandon: I always wanted to work in an office and now here I am! And of course I love earning money!

1 How long will Connor and Brandon be apprentices and what jobs do they hope to get afterwards?
2 Find three reasons why Connor and Brandon like doing their apprenticeships.

B Read the Tips and tricks box and finish these sentences with the correct forms of the verbs in brackets.

1 I love ... (to be) an apprentice.
2 I decided ... (to do) an apprenticeship last year.
3 Do you like ... (to learn) English?
4 What do you want ... (to do) after college?
  – I want ... (to do) an apprenticehip.

C Write some more sentences like those in task B and read them to the class.

I love ...
Last year/week/weekend I decided ...
I (don't) like ...
One day/After college I want ...

→ finally → to decide (to do sth.) → brilliant

Tips and tricks
Auf einige Verben in Englisch folgt ein Infinitiv, auf andere eine *ing*-Form. Beispiele:
to decide / to want + Infinitiv (to do)
to like / to love + *ing*-Form (doing)

Am Ende von Unit 7 kann ich:
— über Arbeiten und Arbeitsstellen sprechen und schreiben,
— Ausdrücke wie *to want to do sth* und *to like doing sth* richtig verwenden.

Unit 7 Starting work

| Check-in | Training | More please! | Check-out |

2 Working as a retail assistant

This is Holly. She is also English and she also has an apprenticeship. She is a trainee retail assistant in a store which is part of a large national chain. She is talking about her apprenticeship and being at work for the first time.

R, I, P
A 2.19

A Listen and put the pictures A-F below in the correct order. Compare with a partner and report to the class.

The first picture is picture …

A
Managers in a meeting

Logistics – goods in a warehouse

B

C
A till

D
Advertising and marketing

E
A window display

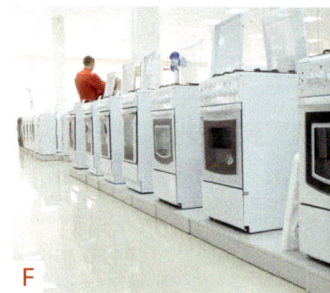

F
Domestic goods in a retail store

→ retail   → manager   → till   → display (to display)   → logistics

68

R **B Listen again and choose the correct answer a, b or c.**

1 Holly will be an apprentice for another
 a year.
 b two years.
 c four years.

2 Holly decided to go into retail work
 a last year.
 b in her last year at school.
 c when she was a child.

3 Holly says that working in a store is … than she expected.
 a easier
 b more interesting
 c more complicated

4 Holly says that goods on display in a shop must look attractive and
 a not be too expensive.
 b not be too close together.
 c be easy to find.

5 Holly says that logistics are … for retail businesses.
 a quite important
 b extremely important
 c not that important

6 Holly finds advertising and marketing
 a really interesting.
 b simple.
 c not as interesting as other aspects of her work.

7 Holly wants
 a to stay in her store for many years.
 b to try other jobs before she finally chooses retail work.
 c to become a manager one day.

P **C Here are some sentences that Holly said. Look at grammar section 13 at the back of your book and complete the sentences with the correct forms of the verbs (infinitive or *ing*-form).** → More please! A – D

1 And, of course, I love *shopping* (to shop).
2 First, you have to learn … (to operate) the tills.
3 I hate … (to go) into shops where you can never find what you want.
4 That means … (to order) goods, … (to store) them in warehouses, and then … (to deliver) them to stores.
5 I want … (to stay) in retail work and one day I would like … (to become) a manager.

→ complicated → to operate sth → aspect (of sth)

Check-in Training More please! Check-out

3 Starting work

You find this article in a magazine. Read it and do the tasks on page 71.

Starting work: our top tips

Your first days at work are the start of a new part of your life. You're no longer at school (although you may be an apprentice who goes to college one or
5 two days a week), you're now 'a worker', someone with a job and best of all, a wage. It's exciting but you probably feel a bit nervous, too – after all, there will be many things that are new and strange at
10 first. So here are our top tips for those first days at work.

1 Sleep well
You need to be wide awake on your first day. There will be a lot to learn and
15 remember, so make sure you get a good night's sleep. Then make sure you sleep well for the first weeks after that. Having a job and working means having a new routine, very different from your routine at
20 school or college. And expect to be tired at first: you will find the work quite hard when you start working every day.

2 Have the right clothes
Different jobs mean different clothes,
25 maybe even a uniform, and there aren't many jobs where jeans and a T-shirt are the right thing to wear. Find out what is right in your new workplace.

3 Practise travelling to your job
30 You don't want to be late on your first day, so do the journey to your new workplace a couple of times before you start. Traffic can be bad first thing in the morning and the journey can take longer than you expect.

Don't be late on your first day!

35 It's no good telling your new boss your bus was late – all the other workers arrived at work on time.

4 Smile
It's that big moment when you enter your
40 new workplace for the very first time. Take a deep breath and smile. First impressions last a long time so you want to look friendly and enthusiastic when people meet you. And don't forget to be polite – to
45 everyone.

5 If you don't know something, ask
You're here to learn to do a job and one important way to do that is to ask questions. Don't be afraid to ask.
50 People know that you are new – and an apprentice. As someone once said: "There's no such thing as a stupid question." The more you ask, the more you will learn.

→ to mean   → to expect   → traffic   → (first) impression(s)   → there's no such thing (as)

6 Be reliable

Of all the qualities that employers look for in a new worker, at the top of the list is usually that they are 'reliable'. You're at work, remember, not on holiday with your friends. Be punctual for everything: arrive on time in the morning, don't come back late after lunch, be on time for meetings. Do the work that people give you as well as you can (and if there's a problem, ask for help). And if you promise to do something, do it. Try to be a person who people can trust.

7 Learn to get on with people

If all goes well, you will work in your job for a long time and you will see the same people every day. In every workplace there are sometimes problems and very often these are problems with co-workers. Get to know people and learn to get on well with them. Talking and listening are always the best answer. If there's a problem you can't solve like that, then talk to someone who can help. As an apprentice, you normally have a 'mentor'. Try to find solutions. Conflict is never the right answer.

Conflict is never the best way to solve problems!

R, I **A True or false? Write down T or F. Compare with a partner and report to the class.** → More please! E – G

1 According to the article, starting work will mean many changes in your life and at first, working will be quite hard.
2 You can usually wear what you want at work.
3 Bosses usually understand if you have a problem (e.g. with traffic) when you come to work in the morning.
4 The writer of the article says that people get an idea about us when they first meet us and they have this idea for a long time.
5 According to the text, we should try not to ask too many questions at work because people will find us 'stupid'.
6 In the opinion of the writer, one of the most important things at work is that people learn to trust you.
7 What should you do if you have a problem at work with a co-worker? The writer says you should go first to your boss or 'mentor' for help.

M **B Your friend plans to start a new job soon and is interested in this article – but (s)he doesn't speak English very well. Give the main ideas of the text in German.**

→ reliable   → (to be) on time   → to trust sb.   → to get on (well) with sb.   → to solve (a problem)   → mentor

Unit 7 Starting work 71

4 More please!

A *Ing*-form: spelling → Grammar 13

Copy the table and write in the *ing*-forms of the verbs.

Verb	ing-form	Verb	ing-form
to work	*working*	to learn	?
to do	*doing*	to go	?
to write	?	to operate	?
to cut	?	to sit	?
to play	?	to stay	?
to listen	?	to deliver	?
to begin	?	to travel	?
to die	?	to tie	?

B To like + *ing*-form → Grammar 13

Use the *ing*-forms from your table in task A to complete these sentences. You don't need to use all the verbs.

1 I like *learning* English.
2 But I don't like ... homework.
3 I like ... to music.
4 At the weekend, I like ... in bed in the morning.
5 I don't like ... to the dentist.
6 Do you like ... football?
7 I like ... by train but buses are boring.

C Verbs + infinitive, verbs + *ing*-form → Grammar 13

Choose the correct form of the verb to complete the sentences.

1 I love to be / *being* an apprentice.
2 When I leave college, I want to get / getting an apprenticeship in a retail store.
3 I hate to get / getting up in the morning.
4 One day I would like to have / having my own company.
5 You have to learn to do / doing lots of new things when you first start work.
6 When did you decide to do / doing an apprenticeship?
7 You want to do / doing well in your exams, right? Well, that means to work / working hard in all your lessons.
8 I like to play / playing football, but I prefer to play / playing tennis.

I think he wants to come in.

P ▲ **D Verbs + infinitive, verbs + *ing*-form** → Grammar 13

Complete the sentences with the correct forms of the verbs. Be careful of spellings.

1 This is Will. He is also doing a retail apprenticeship. He didn't like *being* (to be) at school, but he likes ... (to work) and of course he loves ... (to have) money in his pocket at the end of the month.
2 Will always wanted ... (to work) in a shop, even when he was a kid.
3 He decided ... (to do) an apprenticeship two years ago.
4 As an apprentice, Will is learning ... (to do) lots of new things.
5 In his free time, Will enjoys ... (to listen) to music so he really likes ... (to work) in the music section of the big department store where he is an apprentice.
6 He likes ... (to travel) so the in-store travel agency is also interesting for him.
7 Will's managers are really pleased with him and one day, Will would like ... (to become) a manager himself. That means ... (to put in) a lot of effort every day and always ... (to do) his best.

R, P △ **E Verbs + infinitive, verbs + *ing*-form** → Grammar 13

1 Choose the correct form of the verb to finish these sentences. In one sentence both forms are possible.

a Listen, please. You need *to remember* / remembering this.
b You can't expect to be / being successful in life if you don't work hard.
c When did you start to work / working here?
d Where do you want to work / working when you finish your apprenticeship? Would you like to stay / staying here?
e It's no good to say / saying you don't know what to do. You can always ask me for help.
f Don't forget to put / putting the lights off when you leave the office.
g If you promise to do / doing something, then you must do it.
h I'm trying to understand / understand this, but it's really hard.

2 Now finish these sentences with the correct form of the verb.

a Tomorrow, you'll learn ... (to use) our computer network.
b Do you like ... (to use) computers?
c Why did you decide ... (to work) here?
d What do you enjoy ... (to do) in your free time?

Check-in | Training | **More please!** | Check-out

P ▲ **F Verbs + infinitive, verbs + *ing*-form** → Grammar 13

Complete the sentences with the correct forms of the verbs. Be careful of spellings!

1 Now that I have a job, I can afford .... (to buy) a car.
2 I'm afraid I can't stand .... (to watch) football on TV.
3 Why did you choose .... (to do) an apprenticeship?
4 My teacher suggested .... (to work) part-time to get some work experience.
5 One day, I hope .... (to travel) to the USA.
6 If you practise .... (to write) sentences like these, you will soon learn .... (to use) verbs with infinitives and *ing*-forms.
7 She is a vegetarian. She gave up .... (to eat) meat a year ago.
8 There's no point in .... (to go) to the gym tomorrow. It will be closed.

P ▲ **G Verbs + infinitive, verbs + *ing*-form** → Grammar 13

Finish these sentences in your own words and with your own ideas.

1 I love …
2 I also enjoy …
3 I don't mind …
4 But I hate …
5 One day, I want …
6 I often forget …
7 I can't imagine …
8 I think everyone should try …
9 There's no point in …

What are you into?

R, P ▲ **H Key words**

Find the correct words and phrases at the bottom of pages 67–71 and complete these sentences. The words that you need are not in the same order as on the pages!

1 You can pay for these goods at the .... over there.
2 What's your first .... of the new apprentice?
3 It's important to be .... : always be on time, and if you promise to do something, always do it.
4 Leave the house early today – the .... on the motorway is really bad this morning.
5 .... is 'Einzelhandel' in German.
6 Your window .... looks very good. I think lots of customers will come into the shop when they see it.
7 I didn't .... to see Mike at the party. It was a big surprise.
8 First, second, next, then, and .... !

5 Now you

P, I   **A Choose one of the activities below.**

1 Make a word web about 'work'. You can do this in a small group and produce a poster to show to the class with a gallery walk. There are some ideas below to get you started.

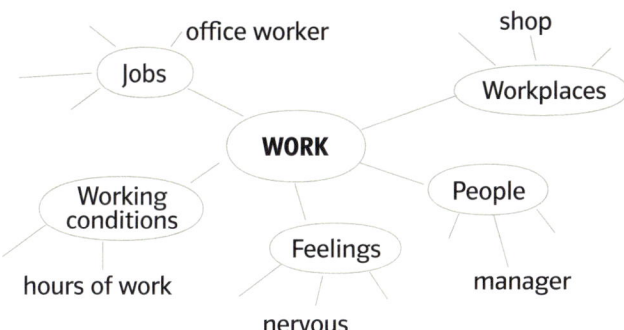

2 Work with a partner. Write a conversation about a job that you had – a part time job, for example, or a short work placement. Read your conversation to the class. Please look now at page 77.

V7

Video Lounge Starting a new job

R, P   **Maya is starting her work placement at the hotel in Berlin. Watch and answer the questions.**

1 Who is the first person Maya meets at the hotel?
2 When does Mr Xiao want to stay at the hotel?
3 What sort of room would he like?
4 What does Maya forget to do in her conversation with Mr Xiao?
5 She calls him back and he gives her some details. Note down this information.
6 What does Maya give the man at the end?

Partner files
Job pages
Test

Partner files | Job pages | Test

PARTNER FILES

Unit 7 [5 Now you]

Make a conversation with your partner about a job that you had. You can use the role cards below, but if you had a real job, you can talk about that.

1 Choose one of the role cards below.
2 Copy the table below the role cards and complete it with information from your role card (or about your real job).
3 Prepare questions for your partner, then interview her/him and make notes.
   When/Where did you…?
   What sorts of things did you do?
   How did you feel?/What did you learn?
3 Write a conversation in which you take it in turns to ask and talk about your job.
4 Read your conversation to the class.

ROLE CARD A
In your summer holidays last year you had a part time job for five weeks in a supermarket. You worked four days a week from 1 o'clock until 6 o'clock in the afternoon. You were a checkout assistant – that means you worked at a checkout where customers pay for their goods. You were often tired at first and sometimes you didn't want to go to work in your holidays, but your co-workers were really friendly and you made some new friends. It was also good to learn about the world of work. And the money which you earned was great! You would like to work there again, perhaps next Christmas.

ROLE CARD B
Last October you had a work placement for two weeks in a multiplex cinema. You worked six days a week in the afternoon or evening each day. You saw lots of different parts of work in a cinema – in the box office (where they sell tickets), in the shop (where they sell popcorn,etc.), in the projection room (where there is the projector which shows the films) and in the office (where they look after the cinema's money, advertise the films, etc.). You found the work experience fascinating and you learned a lot about the real world of work. It was also good working in a team with other people. Now you would love to work in a cinema one day.

when?/how long?	?
where?	?
hours/days?	?
tasks at work?	?
feelings and experiences?	?
learn?	?

Partner files 77

Partner files | **Job pages** | Test

JOB PAGES

Phoning at work (Unit 1)

People use the phone all the time at work and even if you work in Germany, many phone calls today are in English. Dominik Hamann is a German businessman. He is at the airport in Germany on his way to London on a business trip. He is calling three business contacts in England before he flies.

R, P
A 2.21

A Here is the list of people who Mr Hamann wants to speak to and their companies. Listen to the three conversations. What happens? Can he speak to the people or is there perhaps a problem?

1 David James – TechArt Web Design Ltd
2 Liz Williams – Premier Advertising UK Ltd
3 Pete Marsh – Hobart Logistics

R, P

B Now listen again to the three conversations and note down the missing words and phrases.

Conversation 1

Receptionist   Hamann   James

Receptionist: TechArt Web Design. Good morning.
Hamann: Good morning. **(1)** ... David James, please?
Receptionist: Who is calling please?
Hamann: It's Dominik Hamann from HB Exports in Germany.
Receptionist: **(2)** ... Mr Hamann, I'm putting you through now.
James: Dominik, hi. How are you?
Hamann: Hi, David. **(3)** ... . I'm at the airport in Germany. I just wanted to give you a quick call before I arrive in England …

78

Conversation 2

Receptionist   Hamann
Premier Advertising, Craig Lewis speaking. **(4)** ... ?
　　　　Hello. Can I speak to Liz Williams, please? This is Dominik Hamann from HB Exports in Germany.
I'm sorry, Mr Hamann, Liz is **(5)** ... at the moment. Will you hold?
　　　　Sure. Thanks.

Conversation 3

Receptionist   Hamann
Hobart Logistics. Good morning. Sally speaking.
　　　　Good morning. Can I speak to Pete Marsh, please?
I'm sorry but Mr Marsh **(6)** ... at the moment. He should be back in about half an hour. Will you call back or can he call you?
　　　　I'll call back later, thanks.
Can I take **(7)** ..., please?
　　　　Yes, it's Dominik Hamann from HB Exports in Germany.
Thanks, Mr Hamann. I'll tell Mr Marsh **(8)** ...
　　　　Thanks. Bye now.
Goodbye.

P, I　**C　Now YOU. Work in small groups to make your own conversations.**

1. Copy and complete the diagram below with the key phrases from the three conversations. Compare your diagrams in class. Make sure you know the German meanings of all the phrases (you can make a list of English and German phrases side by side).
2. In your group, choose two of the conversations above and write your own. Invent names, company names, etc. yourselves.
3. Read your conversations to the class – or record them and play the recordings.

Receptionist: Good morning ...
Caller:　　　 Could I speak to ...

Receptionist: One moment ...
...

Receptionist: I'm sorry ...
...

Receptionist: I'm sorry ...
...

Job pages　79

| Partner files | **Job pages** | Test

Preparing for a meeting (Unit 2)

This is Amrit Dhillon, an admin assistant in a company in Scotland. The company makes and sells clothing. Amrit has many different tasks as an admin assistant. One of them is preparing for the meetings that take place in the company's offices. So what does she have to do? How do you prepare for a meeting?

R **A** Look at the picture below and read the notes below and on the next page.

A. A meeting room.
First, Amrit has to organise a room for the meeting. There are three meeting rooms in her company's offices, all with a table in the centre and chairs around the table. But there are different meetings all the time, and lots of people want to use the rooms. Amrit has to find a meeting room that is free and book it for the day and time when her bosses want to have their meeting.

B. Documents.
The most important document for a meeting is the agenda and this is normally sent to people before the meeting. In the meeting itself, there can also be handouts – enough copies, of course, for everyone.

C./D. Equipment.
When people make a presentation or want to explain something, they need equipment – like the whiteboard in a classroom. Another piece of equipment can be a flipchart like the one in this picture. In modern offices, there is also often digital equipment like multi-media projectors (what you call 'beamers' in Germany) and a screen. And finally many companies nowadays have video conferences with cameras and microphones and a large video screen.

E. Refreshments.
So now there is a room, the necessary documents, and equipment for presentations. The last thing that is needed is refreshments – coffee, water, fruit juices, maybe also biscuits. People work better when they have nice refreshments!

P **B** Describe the picture on the opposite page. What is happening? What can you see?

The picture shows some people who are in a meeting.
They are sitting … / One man is …
He is making a …
On the left / the right you can see …
In the centre / foreground / …
On the table …

P **C** Last week, Amrit got this email from her boss, Richard. Read the email and make a to-do list for Amrit. Put the things she has to do in what you think is the right order.

> Hi Amrit
>
> I want to have a meeting next week with my sales team. It will last about three hours on Wednesday morning if there is a room free (start at 9.30 am). I'll send you the agenda tomorrow. There'll also be some handouts for everyone. I want to make a presentation at the meeting – the information etc. I need is on my laptop. One last thing, it's Harry Martin's birthday on Wednesday so some cakes or similar would be nice. Thanks!
>
> Richard

| Partner files | **Job pages** | Test |

Business correspondence 1: an enquiry (Unit 3)

Germany is famous for its precision engineering. Otto Wolff Gartengeräte GmbH, which is based in Wuppertal, makes a range of garden equipment including lawn mowers. The firm exports its products around the world but one of its biggest markets is Great Britain – the British love gardening! Grigori Skorikov (below) works in Wolff's EU export department. Today he has an email from a British company. The email is an enquiry.

R, P **A** You can see the email on the next page. Look at it now. Copy and complete the table below with information from the email.

ENQUIRY: received 21 March 20...	
company name	?
address / country	?
writer's name	?
company's business (what does the company do?)	?
size of company	?
What WOLFF product(s) is the writer interested in?	?
send (information / catalogue etc.)	?

M **B** Grigori's boss is Frau Lindner. She is the manager of the EU export department. Write a short email to her in German in which you summarise the key points of the enquiry.

> Liebe Frau Lindner,
>
> heute haben wir eine E-Mail von ... erhalten.
> ...

82

Von: c.mitchell@swallows-gardencentres.co...uk
An: info@wolffgarten...de
Betreff: Enquiry

Dear Sirs

We saw your lawnmowers at the trade fair in London last week and would like further information.

Swallows Garden Centres Ltd is a company based in Oxford in the south of England. We are a national chain of over 30 garden centres around Britain. You can visit our website and find out more about us at www.swallows-gardencentres.co...uk.

If your prices are competitive, we may want to buy quantities of your products for our garden centres. Please send us your current catalogue and price list. We would also like to know about any discounts that you can offer us, your terms of payment, and how quickly you can deliver quantity orders.

I look forward to hearing from you soon.
Yours sincerely

Charlotte Mitchell – Purchasing Manager
Swallows Garden Centres Ltd, 75 Banbury Road, Oxford OX1 3JJ

R, M **C** Look carefully at the email and make a list of phrases that you can use in an enquiry. There are some phrases below to get you started. Give the German translations for your phrases, then compare your lists in class.

Dear Sirs	Sehr geehrte Damen und Herren,
We saw your products at a trade fair / on your website.	Wir haben Ihre Produkte auf einer Messe / auf Ihrer Webseite gesehen.
We would like further information.	Wir hätten gern weitere Informationen.
We are a ... (company) ... (country)	Wir sind ein ... Unternehmen in ...
If your prices are competitive, we may want to order quantities of your products.	...
...	...

P, I **D** Now YOU. Work with a partner or in a small group. You are a German supermarket chain. Last week you saw some English biscuits at a trade fair in Cologne and would like more information about them. The English firm's email address is info@wilsonsbiscuits.co...uk. Write an email enquiry.

Business correspondence 2: an offer (Unit 4)

Grigori Skorikov works for a company in Wuppertal which makes and sells garden machines. Yesterday, he received an enquiry from a chain of garden centres in Britain. They wanted details about Grigori's firm's lawnmowers. Today, Grigori is writing a reply. He is making the British company an offer.

R, P **A** You can see Grigori's email on the next page. Look at it now and at the box below and say if the statements are true or false. Correct the false statements.

Understanding offers
Incoterms
Diese Klauseln werden im internationalen Handel verwendet und sagen dir, was ein Preis beinhaltet. DDP steht für 'Delivered Duty Paid' (Geliefert verzollt) - der Preis beinhaltet die Lieferung zum Lager des Käufers und jedwede Einfuhrsteuer.

Discounts
Firmen gewähren oft Rabatte, wenn ein Käufer mehr als eine bestimmte Menge an Waren kauft: ein ‚Mengenrabatt'.

Terms of payment
Diese sind von Bedeutung, wenn der Käufer für die Waren zahlt, z.B. wenn er/sie bestellt oder innerhalb von 30 Tagen nach Erhalt der Rechnung.

Valid for …
Wie lange das Angebot unverändert bleibt.

1 Grigori sends Wolff's catalogue and price list by post to the firm in England.
2 The English company must pay the cost of transporting the goods from Germany to Oxford.
3 If the English firm buys more than 50 lawnmowers, they will pay less than the normal price.
4 The English firm can pay for the lawnmowers when they arrive at their warehouse in Oxford.
5 The English firm will get the lawnmowers ten days after they order them.
6 The English firm doesn't have to buy lawnmowers immediately. The prices and conditions will stay the same for three months.

An: c.mitchell@swallows-gardencentres.co...uk
Betreff: Your enquiry

Dear Ms Mitchell

Many thanks for your enquiry of 21 March about our lawnmowers. We are pleased to make you the following offer. Attached are our product catalogue and current price list as PDF documents. All our prices are DDP Oxford. We can offer you a volume discount of 5% on all orders over 50 items. For first orders we normally require payment in full with your order. We will dispatch your order within 10 working days of receipt of your payment.

This offer is valid for three months.

Thank you again for your interest in our products and I look forward to receiving your order.

Yours sincerely

Grigori Skorikov

EU export department
Otto Wolff Gartengeräte GmbH
An der Seilbahn 35
42105 Wuppertal
Germany

B You work in the offices in a company in Germany which makes aromatic wax candles. Your boss, Frau Thönes, received an enquiry yesterday from a large store in London and wants to reply to the store with an offer. Frau Thönes gives you these notes. Write the email.

Bitte verfasse und versende die folgende Email.
An: Jane Archer at Lyons Foods Ltd, London:
(j.archer@lyonsfoods.co...uk)
- *danke für Ihre Anfrage vom 17. Juni*
- *wir freuen uns, Ihnen das folgende Angebot machen zu können*
- *unser aktueller Katalog ist beigefügt (als PDF)*
- *alle Preise sind DDP London*
- *Mengenrabatt von 10 % für Bestellungen über 10 000 Euro*
- *wir verlangen die Zahlung innerhalb von 30 Tagen nachdem Sie die Bestellung erhalten haben*
- *dieses Angebot gilt für einen Monat*
- *ich hoffe/wir hoffen, bald von Ihnen zu hören*

Business correspondence 3: an order (Unit 5)

A British company called Swallows Garden Centres is thinking of buying some lawnmowers from a firm in Germany called Otto Wolff Gartengeräte. A couple of days ago, Charlotte Mitchell, the purchasing manager at Swallows, received an offer from Wolff. She decides to buy some lawnmowers and today she is sending an order. She completes a purchase order form and writes a letter to send with it.

PURCHASE ORDER No. 1249   DATE: 23/03/20..

CAT No.	ITEM	QTY	PRICE	AMOUNT
RM100	Large lawn mower	10	450	4,500
RM50	Medium lawn mower	20	250	5,000
RM25	Small lawn mower	50	125	6,250
			SUBTOTAL	15,750
		LESS 5% QUANTITY DISCOUNT		787.50
			TOTAL €	14,962.50

Date: 23 March 20..

Otto Wolff GmbH
An der Seilbahn 35
42105 Wuppertal
Germany

Dear Mr Skorikov

Purchase order No. 1249

Thank you for your offer of 21 March. Please find enclosed our purchase order.

We note that your prices include a 5% quantity discount for orders over 50 items and that the prices are DDP Oxford, England. We also note that for a first order you require payment in full with our order and we have today made a bank transfer to you of €14,962.50.

The consignment will be dispatched within 10 days of receipt of our payment.

Yours sincerely

Charlotte Mitchell
Charlotte Mitchell
Purchasing Manager

Encl: Purchase order No. 1249

A Look at Charlotte's letter and the order form on the last page. Find the English for the following German words and phrases. Be careful! Sometimes the answer can be an abbreviation (Abkürzung).

1 Datum
2 Katalog (Nummer)
3 Menge
4 Zwischensumme
5 anbei finden Sie
6 wir stellen fest, dass
7 wir haben Ihnen heute einen Betrag von … überwiesen
8 innerhalb von 10 Tagen nach unserem Zahlungseingang
9 Mit freundlichen Grüßen

B Now YOU. Work in a small group. You work for a large German department store. Last month you saw some British clothing at a trade fair. It is made by a firm called Glasgow Mill in Glasgow, Scotland. You wrote an enquiry to them and got an offer last week. Now you want to order some clothes (shirts, pullovers, dresses, trousers, etc.). Write a letter and fill out a purchase order (think of the items and prices yourselves). Below you can see what the British firm offered you. Your contact is Mrs Linda MacDonald.

- all prices DDP Dusseldorf
- quantity discount on orders over € 50,000
- payment in full with first order
- dispatch within 30 days of receipt of order

Partner files | **Job pages** | Test

Business correspondence 4: a complaint (Unit 6)

In March this year, Grigori Skorikov's company Otto Wolff Gartengeräte began selling lawnmowers to a British company, Swallows Garden Centres Ltd. Over the next three months, all went very well and Swallows bought many more mowers. But today Grigori has an email from his contact in the British company, Charlotte Mitchell. There is a problem. The email is a complaint.

M **A** Look at Charlotte Mitchell's email. You are Grigori. Write a short email in German to your boss Frau Lindner in which you explain the problem.

R, P **B** If your firm makes a mistake (like Grigori's), here are some tips. Look at the tips and at Grigori's email. Why did Grigori write certain things? What phrases did he use?

Complaints: What to do
Things can go wrong in business. It's normal!
- If it's your mistake, accept responsibility.
- Apologise (say sorry) – more than once if necessary.
- Give a reason for your mistake (say what happened).
- Tell your customer clearly what to do (send back the goods, keep/ destroy the goods etc.).
- You don't want to lose your customer, so (if you can) offer them something extra. 'Good will' is very, very important in business.

What Grigori does	Phrase(s)
He accepts responsibility.	*It's clearly our fault*
…	…

Von: c.mitchell@swallows-gardencentres.co...uk
An: g.skorikov@ottowolff...de
Betreff: Our order number 4464

Dear Grigori

I'm writing about our order number 4464. The consignment arrived yesterday but when we unpacked the container we found that it contained the wrong goods: there were lots of garden tools but no lawnmowers. This is a real problem for us as June is one of our busiest months in our centres.

Could you therefore please send us replacements very urgently and let us know what you would like us to do with the tools?

Kind regards
Charlotte

An: c.mitchell@swallows-gardencentres.co...uk
Betreff: Your order number 4464

Dear Charlotte

I'm extremely sorry to hear there was a mistake with your order number 4464. It's clearly our fault. We're always careful with our orders but this time there was a mix up in our dispatch department. Please accept my apologies.

I'm today dispatching your order again by express carrier. It should arrive tomorrow afternoon.

Please return the faulty container to us at our expense. In addition, please also accept a 30% discount on your next order with us to show our good will.

Please let me know when the new order arrives and once again, sorry for our mistake.

Kind regards
Grigori

C Now YOU. Work with a partner. You work for different companies, one in Germany and one in another country (Britain, the Netherlands, the USA etc.). Write and exchange emails – think of the details yourselves.

| Partner files | **Job pages** | Test |

Understanding advertisements (Unit 7)

Holly is an apprentice in an electrical store in England. It is called Homestore and for the next two weeks her store will have a promotion – they will sell lots of products on special offer. This weekend, Homestore will put a leaflet in all the local papers to advertise the promotion. You can see the leaflet on the next page.

P, I **A** With a partner, look at the leaflet and the notes HOW AN ADVERTISING LEAFLET WORKS below. Then use the phrases to explain how the leaflet 'works'. Give a short talk to the class.

> ### HOW AN ADVERTISING LEAFLET WORKS
>
> **1.** The leaflet must quickly 'grab attention' (Look at me!). A picture, bold colours and big letters are common ways to do this. (Did you know? People decide to read – or not to read – an advertisement in the first three seconds!)
>
> **2.** Now the person who is looking at the leaflet must want to read more – you have to interest the person. A question (or question) is a good way to do this.
>
> **3.** People like to think the advertisement is for them personally. Speak directly to the reader and use the words *you, your,* etc as often as you can.
>
> **4.** Reading the leaflet is not enough. People must also do something – buy your products! They must see how to do this. So tell them your name and when they can shop. Firms also often say: Buy now!
>
> **5.** Many firms have a slogan. These words always appear with the name of your firm. When people see your name, they think of the slogan.

First, the leaflet must 'grab attention'. Homestore does this with …
Homestore wants people to be interested in the promotion and it uses … to do this.
The writer of the leaflet speaks directly to the readers. For example, …
So what must the reader do? The leaflet gives …

P, I **B** Now YOU. Work in small groups to write a leaflet for a product (or service) that you know about. Use the techniques above and present your leaflet to the class.

Save up to £300!

Hurry! Ends 31 March!

**Do you need a new cooker?
Is your old fridge, well, old!?
How about a new, bigger TV or
one of the latest vacuum cleaners?**

**We have hundreds of products in store
at LOW, LOW prices! You could save £300!**

But hurry! Offers end on 31 March.

HOMESTORE
Britain's favourite electrical store

**We're open
Weekdays 8 am — 8 pm
Sunday 9 am — 4 pm**

f Visit us on Facebook!

TEST
1 Reading

You find this article in an English language magazine. Read the text and do the tasks which follow.

Hi! I'm here for the job interview.

Me, too.

What do you think? Who would get the job?

OK, you don't have to be a genius to answer that question. If you went to an interview with an employer in a baseball cap, you most probably wouldn't get the job – or only if it was as a baseball player. But there are lots more dos and don'ts for job interviews. This month we give you…

15 hot tips for the perfect job interview!

Before the interview…
1. Do your homework. Find out as much as you can about the company that you are applying to for a job. There are lots of ways to do this. If it is a shop, go into its stores and look around. Even better, for any company nowadays, there is always lots of information online – the company's own website, of course, or news about it.
2. Find out exactly where the interview will take place and plan your journey. Being late for a job interview is definitely not acceptable. If you can, practise the journey before the interview and remember that traffic can be worse at different times of the day.
3. One of the most important ways to prepare for an interview is to make a list of the questions that the interviewer may ask you. And then to write out some answers. Some people also like to practise an interview with a friend or family member.
4. Go to bed early and get a good sleep the night before!

At the interview…
5. Don't be late! In fact, plan to arrive early – 15–20 minutes, say – even if this means you have to wait around outside.
6. Yes, wear nice, clean, simple clothes. You don't have to look like a fashion model or a rich businessperson, but you must be smart. This also includes your hair, and if you are a woman, your make-up (if you wear it). You and your friends may love your pink hair and the ring in your nose, but most employers won't.
7. First impressions are always important. Shake hands with the interviewer and smile. Be positive and friendly.
8. Wait until the interviewer asks you to sit down, then during the interview sit upright at all times. You aren't at home on the sofa in front of the TV!
9. Look at the interviewer when (s)he asks questions and when you answer. This is called eye contact and it is very important. We often think that a person who doesn't look at us is not honest (is hiding something).

10 Answer the questions but don't talk too much. The interviewer has lots of questions to go through and if you give 20-minute answers, that won't be possible (and will be very boring!).
11 Even if you feel nervous, speak clearly and not too quickly.
12 Tell the truth. This may sound strange, but sometimes it is easy to want to impress the interviewer with facts about you that are not true. If you tell a lie, it is very likely that the interviewer will find out (if not now, then later), and that could lose you the job.
13 Be honest in another way, too. If you don't understand a question, just say so. This is not a sign that you are stupid – in fact, it is an intelligent thing to do.
14 Very important! Interviewers almost always end an interview with words like: 'Do you have any questions for me?' Prepare two or three things you can ask.
15 And finally, thank the interviewer, smile again, and leave the room quietly.

605 words

A Read the statements below. Write down if a statement is true (T), false (F), or that the information is not in the text (NIT).

1 It is not generally a good idea to wear a baseball cap for a job interview.
2 Listing possible questions is OK but not the best way to prepare for an interview.
3 When you first meet the interviewer you should say 'hello' and use their name.
4 An interviewer will get a bad impression of you if you don't look at her or him directly.
5 Two to three minutes is the perfect length for your answers to interview questions.
6 You must never tell a lie in an interview.
7 You may look stupid if you tell an interviewer that you don't understand a question.
8 It isn't just interviewers who can ask questions, a candidate can often ask them, too.

B Complete the sentences with information from the text.

1 One of the best ways to find out about a company before an interview is to look …
2 You must know where to go for your interview and if possible …
3 It is always better to arrive … for an interview than to arrive late.
4 The right clothes are important but … are important, too.
5 It is important to answer questions but you mustn't …
6 People are often nervous in interviews – that's normal. However, you must still be careful to…
7 The last things to do at the end of the interview are to…

→ *upright:* aufrecht   → *to impress sb:* jmdn beeindrucken

Partner files | Job pages | **Test**

2 Listening

A 2.22

You will hear part of a radio programme from New Zealand called *Jobs around the world*. The presenter, Mike Smith, is interviewing two young people from Germany. You will hear each interview twice.

INTERVIEW 1 Listen to the interview with Julia Lammert and choose the right answer a, b, c or d.

1 Julia is
   a a kindergarten teacher.
   b an electrician.
   c a carpenter.
   d a policewoman.

2 She chose her job because
   a her dad is a carpenter.
   b she loved making things as a kid.
   c it was the idea of one of her teachers.
   d her boyfriend is a policeman.

3 After Julia left school
   a she went to college full-time.
   b she got a job.
   c she was unemployed.
   d she got an apprenticeship and went to college part-time.

4 What do her friends think about her job?
   a They were surprised at first but now they think it's great.
   b They think she's crazy.
   c They all say: "You must do what you want."
   d They think it's a bad idea.

5 If Julia hadn't chosen this job, she would maybe have become
   a a fashion model.
   b a secretary.
   c a fashion designer.
   d a shop assistant.

INTERVIEW 2 Listen to the interview with Hasan Samsek. True or false? Write down T or F.

1 Hasan is a care worker who looks after disabled people.
2 At school, he didn't want to be a care worker.
3 After he finished school, he was an apprentice electrician.
4 He wanted to become a care worker after a visit to a care home with his class at school.
5 He believes that men are better care workers than women.

→ *disabled:* behindert

3 Mediation

You work for a company in Germany called Labortek which manufactures laboratory equipment – microscopes, for example. Next week, there will be a visit to your company by some American businesspeople. Below you can see some information about your company. Make notes of the key points in English: you needn't write full sentences.

Firmenname	Labortek GmbH
Hauptsitz und Werk	Fulda, Deutschland
Branche	Herstellung von Laborausstattung
Geschichte	begann 1911, wuchs sehr schnell in den 1960ern und 70ern, jetzt Europas größter Hersteller von Laborausstattung
Internationale Firmensitze	in 16 Ländern weltweit
Angestellte	(Deutschland) 1.800; (weltweit) 2.500

4 Writing

Choose ONE of the tasks below.

1 You are applying to an international company in Germany for an apprenticeship. As part of your application, the firm wants a text of around 150 words about you. Write the text. In it, say:
· your name, age and where you live
· how long you have lived there
· where you are at college and something about your typical day there
· your interests and hobbies in your free time
· the job you want to have in the future and two reasons why you want that job

2 You work in a large hotel in Germany. You regularly buy jams *(Konfitüren)* from a company in England. Your contact in the English company is the export manager, James Ryan (email:j.ryan@toptreejams.co…uk). Normally, the jams arrive quickly and safely, but last week, all the jam jars in the package were broken. Write an email to James to complain about the consignment. Include the following points:
· subject of the email (Betreff)
· a suitable beginning
· the order number for the jams
· exactly what happened
· why this is a problem for you
· you would like replacements
· a suitable ending to the email

Anhang
Grammar summary
Skills files
Vocabulary

GRAMMAR SUMMARY

1 Das simple present

A Allgemein

Das simple present wird verwendet:
- für Aussagen, die längere Zeit gültig sind,
- um auszudrücken, was jemand regelmäßig tut.

I **go** to college five days a week.

I **live** in Germany.

B Mit *sometimes*, *often* usw.

Da man mit dem simple present ausdrückt, was man regelmäßig tut, wird es oft mit Wörtern wie *usually*, *normally*, *sometimes*, *often*, *always*, *never* verwendet. Diese Wörter (Adverbien) stehen immer:
- **vor** einem Vollverb,
- **nach** *to be*.

I **usually** get up at 7 a.m.

I **often** watch TV in the evenings.

I'm **always** happy on Fridays.

C Bildung: Aussagen

Das simple present wird aus der Grundform des Verbs (Infinitiv ohne *to*) gebildet. Nach *he/she/it* endet das Verb immer auf *-s* oder *-es*!

a An die meisten Verben wird einfach *-s* angehängt.
b Die Endung *-es* wird bei Verben benutzt, die auf *s*, *ss*, *x*, *ch*, oder *sh* enden (z. B. *to finish*), da es schwer wäre, nur ein *-s* auszusprechen.
c Auch *to go* und *to do* enden mit *-es*.
d Ein Sonderfall sind Verben, die auf *-y* enden: *to tidy* → *he tid**ies***.

a to work	b to finish
I work	I finish
he/she/it work**s**	he/she/it finish**es**
we work	we finish
you work	you finish
they work	they finish

c to go	d to tidy
I go	I tidy
he/she/it go**es**	he/she/it tid**ies**
we go	we tidy
you go	you tidy
they go	they tidy

D Bildung: Fragen und Verneinungen

- Fragen im simple present werden mit *do* (bei *he/she/it*: *does*) gebildet.
- Verneinungen bildet man mit *don't* (nach *he/she/it*: *doesn't*).

VORSICHT!
Nach *does/doesn't* kommt immer die Grundform des Verbs:
Does he work? (**!** *Does he work~~s~~?*)
She doesn't work. (**!** *She doesn't work~~s~~.*)

Fragen	Verneinungen
Do I work?	I don't work
Does he/she/it wor**k**?	he/she/it doesn't wor**k**
Do we work?	we don't work
Do you work?	you don't work
Do they work?	they don't work

Grammar summary | Skills files | Vocabulary

2 Das present continuous

A Allgemein

Das present continuous benutzt man für Aktivitäten, die gerade im Augenblick des Sprechens stattfinden. Oder auch um ein Bild zu beschreiben. Es wird häufig mit Zeitangaben wie *at the moment* und *right now* verwendet.

> I**'m reading** this text at the moment.
>
> What can you see in this photo?
> – A hairdresser. Right now, she**'s cutting** a customer's hair.

B Mit *this week*, *this month* usw.

Das present continuous kann auch für längere, befristete Handlungen verwendet werden, die gerade stattfinden, benutzt werden, z. B. *this week*, *this month*.

> We**'re visiting** some friends in England this week.
> Julia **is learning** English on a course in London.

C Bildung: Aussagen

Das present continuous wird mit *to be* und Verb + *-ing* gebildet.

I'm he's / she's / it's we're working you're they're	I'm not working she isn't working
	Am I working? Are you working? Are they working?

D Bildung: Fragen und Verneinungen

Fragen und Verneinungen werden mit den Frage- und Verneinungsformen von *to be* gebildet.

Verb + *-ing*: Schreibregeln
- An die meisten Verben wird einfach *-ing* angehängt:
  work – working, *do – doing*.
- Verben, die auf *-e* enden, verlieren das *-e*:
  use – using, *dance – dancing*.
- Kurze Verben, die auf einen Vokal und einen Konsonanten (außer *-y*, *-w* und *-x*) enden, verdoppeln den Konsonanten:
  cut – cutting (aber *play – playing*).
- Längere Verben, die auf einen Vokal und einen Konsonanten enden, verdoppeln den Konsonanten nicht:
  visit – visiting, *deliver – delivering*.
  (Ausnahmen: *travelling*, *beginning*)
- Bei Verben, die auf *-ie* enden, wird
  -ie zu *-y*: *die – dying*

This is Patrick. He lives in England. He goes to an FE college five days a week.

It's 8.30 in the morning. Patrick is going to college by bus.

3 Das simple past

A Allgemein

Das simple past wird verwendet, um Ereignisse in der Vergangenheit zu schildern, die jetzt abgeschlossen sind. Es wird häufig mit Zeitangaben wie *then*, *in 1970*, *last week* und *30 years ago* benutzt.

I bought them yesterday in town.

Cool shorts, Gary. Where did you get them?

B Bildung: Aussagen

- Regelmäßige Verben bilden das simple past mit *-ed*. Diese Form bleibt in allen Personen gleich.
- Unregelmäßige Verben haben Sonderformen im simple past (eine Liste findest du auf dem Klappumschlag). Diese Formen (außer bei *to be*) bleiben ebenfalls in allen Personen gleich.

regelmäßig	unregelmäßig	
to work	**to go**	**to be**
I worked	I went	I **was**
he worked	he went	he was
she worked	she went	she was
it worked	it went	it was
we worked	we went	we **were**
you worked	you went	you were
they worked	they went	they were

C Bildung: Fragen und Verneinungen

- Fragen im simple past werden in allen Personen mit *did* gebildet.
- Verneinungen bildet man durchgehend mit *didn't*.
- *to be* bildet Fragen und Verneinungen im simple past mit eigenen Formen.

VORSICHT!
Nach *did / didn't* steht immer die Grundform des Verbs:
Did he work? (! *Did he worked?*)
She didn't work. (! *She didn't worked.*)

Fragen	Verneinungen
Did I work?	I didn't work
Did he / she / it work?	he / she / it didn't work
Did we work?	we didn't work
Did you work?	you didn't work
Did they work?	they didn't work

to be	
Was I?	I wasn't
Was he / she / it?	he / she / it wasn't
Were we / you / they?	we / you / they weren't

Verb + -ed: Schreibregeln
- An die meisten Verben wird einfach *-ed* angehängt: *work – work**ed***.
- An Verben, die auf *-e* enden, hängt man nur *-d* an: *us**e** – us**ed**, danc**e** – danc**ed***.
- Kurze Verben, die auf einen Vokal (*a, e, i o, u*) und einen Konsonanten (außer *-y, -w* und *-x*) enden, verdoppeln den Konsonanten: *sho**p** – sho**pp**ed, jo**g** – jo**gg**ed*.
- Längere Verben, die auf einen Vokal und einen Konsonanten enden, verdoppeln den Konsonanten nicht: *visi**t** – visi**t**ed, delive**r** – delive**r**ed*. (Ausnahme: *trave**ll**ed*)
- Bei Verben, die auf *-y* enden, wird *-y* zu *-i*: *stud**y** – stud**ied***.

4 Das present perfect

A Allgemein

How long has Julie had that electric guitar?
For about two days.

Mit dem present perfect und *since/for* kann man 'Wie lange'-Fragen *(How long …?)* beantworten.
- *Since* wird mit einem Zeitpunkt (z. B. *2001, 3 January, last year*) benutzt.
- *For* verwendet man für einen Zeitraum (z. B. *two years, six months*).

B Bildung: Aussagen

Das present perfect wird mit *to have* und der 3. Form (Partizip Perfekt) gebildet.
- Regelmäßige Verben (wie *to work*) bilden ihre 3. Form mit *-ed*.
- Unregelmäßige Verben (wie *to go*) haben Sonderformen, die in der Liste auf dem Klappumschlag zu finden sind.

I have (I've) he has (he's) she has (she's) it has (it's) we have (we've) you have (you've) they have (they've)	worked gone

C Bildung: Fragen und Verneinungen

Fragen und Verneinungen werden mit Frage- und Verneinungsformen von *to have* + 3. Form des Verbs gebildet.

Have you worked? Has he worked?
I haven't worked he/she/it hasn't worked we/you/they haven't worked

5 Das past perfect

A Allgemein

Das past perfect wird für ein Ereignis in der Vergangenheit verwendet, das noch vor einem zweiten Ereignis in der Vergangenheit stattfand. Für das länger zurückliegende Ereignis verwendet man das past perfect, für das nicht ganz so lange zurückliegende das simple past. Wir verwenden das past perfect häufig mit *after*.

She **chose** her job after she **had visited** an interesting company.

B Bildung

Das past perfect wird mit *had* + 3. Form (Partizip Perfekt) des Verbs gebildet. Fragen werden auch mit *had*, Verneinungen mit *hadn't* gebildet.

After Jamie had run in the marathon, he went home and went to sleep!

Aussagen	Verneinungen
I had worked he/she/it had worked we/you/they had worked	I hadn't worked he/she/it hadn't worked we/you/they hadn't worked

Fragen
Had I worked? Had he/she/it worked? Had we/you/they worked?

6. Das Futur: *will*

A Allgemein

Will wird für feststehende Ereignisse in der Zukunft sowie für Vorhersagen und Vermutungen verwendet.

> I'**ll have** a family in 10 years.
> She **won't leave** her job when she has a family.

B Bildung

- **Aussagen** werden mit *will* + Grundform des Verbs gebildet. Die Kurzform (*'ll*) wird fast immer beim Sprechen und häufig auch beim Schreiben verwendet.
- **Fragen** bildet man, indem man *will* und das Subjekt tauscht. Hier sind die Kurzformen nicht möglich.
- **Verneinungen** werden mit *won't* + Grundform des Verbs gebildet.

I will (I'll) come	Will I come?
he will (he'll) come	Will he come?
she will (she'll) come	Will she come?
it will (it'll) come	Will it come?
we will (we'll) come	Will we come?
you will (you'll) come	Will you come?
they will (they'll) come	Will they come?

I won't come
he / she / it won't come
we / you / they won't come

7. Das Futur: *going to*

A Allgemein

Going to verwendet man, um über Pläne und Vorhaben zu sprechen: *I'm going to buy a new jacket* entspricht etwa auf Deutsch: „Ich habe vor, eine neue Jacke zu kaufen."

> I'**m going to** move to a new apartment next month.
> **Are** you **going to** leave home?

B Bildung

- **Aussagen** bildet man mit *to be* + *going to* + Hauptverb.
- **Fragen** bildet man mit den Frageformen von *to be* + *going to* + Hauptverb.
- Für **Verneinungen** benutzt man die Verneinung von *to be* + *going to* + Hauptverb.

I'm he's / she's / it's we're / you're / they're	going to	work
Am I Is he / she / it Are we / you / they	going to	work?
I'm not he / she / it isn't we / you / they aren't	going to	work

Will und **going to**

It won't rain tomorrow.

When I'm big, I'm going to be a footballer!

Anhang Grammar summary **101**

8 Modale Hilfsverben: *must, have to, mustn't* und *don't / doesn't have to*

A Allgemein

Mit den modalen Hilfsverben *must, have to, mustn't* und *don't / doesn't have to* wird ausgedrückt, was man tun muss, nicht tun darf und nicht zu tun braucht (nicht tun muss).

- **must / have to**
  In England you must / have to drive on the left.

- **mustn't**
  You mustn't drive on the right!

- **don't / doesn't have to**
  He doesn't have to drive! He has a driver.

Must und *have to* haben etwa die gleiche Bedeutung. Sie drücken aus, was man tun **muss**.	*Mustn't* drückt aus, was man **nicht darf**. **VORSICHT!** *mustn't* bedeutet **nicht** ‚nicht müssen'.	*Don't / Doesn't have to* drückt aus, was man **nicht zu tun braucht**. **VORSICHT!** *don't have to* = nicht müssen

B Bildung: *must* und *have to*

- *Must* bleibt in allen Personen gleich. Auf *must* folgt die Grundform des Verbs.
- *Have to* bildet man mit *to have* + Grundform des Verbs.

must	have to
I must go he / she / it must go we / you / they must go	I have to go he / she / it has to go we / you / they have to go

C Bildung: *mustn't*

Mustn't bleibt ebenfalls bei allen Personen gleich. Auf *mustn't* folgt die Grundform des Verbs.

I mustn't he / she / it mustn't we / you / they mustn't	go

D Bildung: *don't / doesn't have to*

Die Verneinungsform von *have to* bildet man mit *don't / doesn't have to* + Grundform des Verbs.

I don't have to he / she / it doesn't have to we / you / they don't have to	go

9 *If*-Sätze (Bedingungssätze)

A Allgemein

- Ein Bedingungssatz besteht aus einem *if*-Teil und einem Hauptsatz. Der *if*-Teil beschreibt eine Bedingung und der Hauptsatz drückt aus, was passieren wird oder passieren könnte (oder hätte passieren können), wenn diese Bedingung erfüllt wird.
- Bedingungssätze können entweder mit dem *if*-Teil oder mit dem Hauptsatz beginnen. Wenn der *if*-Teil beginnt, steht immer ein Komma vor dem Hauptsatz.
- Es gibt drei Grundtypen von *if*-Sätzen: Typ 1, 2 und 3.

B *If*-Sätze Typ 1:

If you **ask** the robot, it **will clean** the house.
- Typ 1 drückt aus, was unter bestimmten Bedingungen in der Zukunft geschehen wird oder nicht geschehen wird.

If + simple present	will + Verb
If you go to the party,	you'll see Mitch.

C *If*-Sätze Typ 2:

If I **worked** for that company, I **would need** a good qualification.
- Wir benutzen Typ 2, um über eventuelle Situationen zu sprechen oder wenn du zweifelst, dass eine Bedingung erfüllbar ist.
- **VORSICHT!** Anders als im Deutschen darf *would* nur im Hauptsatz, nicht im *if*-Teil stehen.

If + simple past	would(n't) + Verb
If you went to the party,	you would see Mitch.

D *If*-Sätze Typ 3:

If he **had stayed** on the streets, he **would have died**.
- Typ 3 schildert Ereignisse in der Vergangenheit, die hätten passieren können – die aber nicht passiert sind.

If + past perfect	would(n't) have + Partizip Perfekt (3. Form)
If you had gone to the party,	you would have seen Mitch.

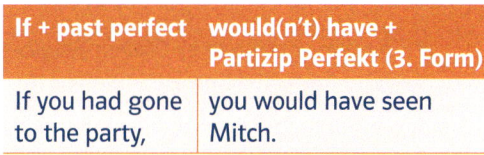

Typ 1: Für Sachen, die passieren werden, wenn …

Typ 2: Für imaginäre, schwer vorstellbare Situationen

Typ 3: Für Sachen, die hätten passieren können

Anhang Grammar summary

10 Das Passiv

A Allgemein: Aktiv- und Passivsätze

- Aktivsätze betonen, **wer** etwas tut. Passivsätze betonen, **was** getan wird – die Handlung steht im Vordergrund.
- In *Kickoff Foundation* findest du nur **Aktivsätze**. In einem Aktivsatz steht das Subjekt vor dem Verb. Gibt es ein Objekt, so steht dieses nach dem Verb.
- **Passivsätze** kann man als ‚umgedrehte' Aktivsätze ansehen: Das Objekt des Aktivsatzes wird zum Subjekt des Passivsatzes.

Aktivsatz		
Subjekt	**Verb**	**Objekt**
The man	bought	the flowers.

Passivsatz		
The man	bought	the flowers.
The flowers	were bought	by the man.

B Bildung

- Das Passiv wird mit *to be* + 3. Form des Verbs (Partizip Perfekt) gebildet.

simple present		simple past	
I'm		I was	
he's		he was	
she's		she was	
it's	made	it was	made
we're		we were	
you're		you were	
they're		they were	

C Mit oder ohne *by*?

Meist wird das Subjekt des Aktivsatzes in einem Passivsatz nicht genannt. Wollen wir aber das Subjekt besonders betonen, können wir es mit Hilfe von *by* am Satzende anfügen. In Satz **a** ist der Name des Regisseurs besonders wichtig. In Satz **b** ist es uninteressant, von wem die Blumen angebaut werden.

a *The film was made **by Steven Spielberg**.*
b *These flowers are grown in **Kenya** (by …).*

They delivered oranges to the supermarket yesterday.

Too many oranges were delivered to the supermarket yesterday!

11 Adjektive und Adverbien

A Allgemein

- **Adjektive** beschreiben Personen und Sachen. Sie stehen meist vor einem Substantiv oder nach *to be*.
- **Adverbien** sagen etwas über Verben aus. Sie sagen uns, **wie** etwas passiert

a **big** robot
The robot is **big**.
The robot loads the lorries **quickly**.

B Adverbien: Bildung

- Ein Adverb wird gebildet, indem *-ly* an das Adjektiv angehängt wird.
- Bei Adjektiven mit der Endung *-y* wird das *-y* zu *-ily*.
- Die Endung *-le* wird zu *-ly*.
- *-ic* wird zu *-ically*.
- Das Adverb von *good* ist *well*.

Adjektiv	Adverb
quick	quick**ly**
easy	eas**ily**
simple	simp**ly**
automatic	automat**ically**
good	well

12 Relativsätze

A Allgemein

Relativsätze sind Sätze, die eines der Relativpronomen *who*, *which* oder *where* enthalten. Sie beschreiben das Wort, auf das sie sich beziehen, näher.

The woman who is helping him is Frau Bliscz.
The document which she has in her hand is Herr Krueger's boarding card.

D *who*, *which* oder *where*?

- *who* für Personen
- *which* für Sachen
- *where* für Orte

A passenger is a person **who** travels by plane.
A plane is a machine **which** carries people.
The place **where** passengers check in is the check-in desk.

Boris can do things very quickly.

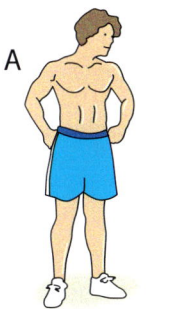
A

B

The guy who goes to a fitness club every day is A or B?

13 Verben + Infinitiv / Verben + *ing*-Form

A Allgemein: Aktiv- und Passivsätze

- Oft verwenden wir zwei Verben hintereinander.
- Im Englischen ist das zweite Verb manchmal ein Infinitiv (to do sth) und manchmal eine *ing*-Form (Verb + -*ing*). Welche von beiden Formen du verwenden musst, hängt vom ersten Verb ab. Auf manche Verben folgt immer ein Infinitiv, auf andere folgt immer eine *ing*-Form. In sehr wenigen Fällen können beide Formen verwendet werden. Es gibt auch ein paar nützliche Ausdrücke, auf die eine *ing*-Form folgt.

1	2	
I want	to learn	Chinese.

1	2	
I love	watching	movies.

B Infinitiv oder *ing*-Form?

- Dies sind die wichtigsten Verben und Ausdrücke, auf die ein Infinitiv oder eine *ing*-Form folgt.

Infinitiv	*ing*-Form
afford	like / enjoy / love / (not)
agree	mind / prefer / dislike /
choose	hate / (can't) stand
decide	
expect	give up
forget	imagine
hope	miss
learn	practise
manage	suggest
need	
promise	**Und die Ausdrücke:**
try	it's no good …
want	there's no point in …
would like	that means…

C Vorsicht!

Auf das Verb *to like* folgt eine *ing*-Form. Aber auf *would like* folgt ein Infinitiv.

I like **swimming**.
I would like **to go** to the USA one day.

D *to begin* und *to start*

Auf diese beiden Verben kann ein Infinitiv oder eine *ing*-Form folgen, ohne dass sich die Bedeutung verändert.

It started **to rain**.
OR:
It started **raining**.

SKILLS FILES
1 Einen längeren Text verstehen

Vor dem Lesen:
1. Woher kommt der Text: Zeitung? Sachbuch? Roman? … ?
2. Handelt es sich um einen Sachtext oder um einen fiktionalen Text?
3. Was erwartest du, wenn du die Bilder und den Titel ansiehst? Wird der Text sachlich, spannend, informativ, … sein?
4. Weißt du etwas über den Autor und die Zeit, in der der Text spielt bzw. geschrieben wurde?

Beim ersten Lesen:
Lies den Text. Ist er so, wie du erwartet hast? Was ist anders?

Beim zweiten Lesen:
Wie kannst du die Bedeutung der neuen Wörter erschließen?

A crazy idea!
For centuries stories about UFOs and aliens have attracted people: Spaceships land on the Earth, people go out to take photos and never **return**, aliens enter the **brains** of people and control their bodies, **hideous** creatures try to **take control of** our world. Many people all over the world believe that there are aliens on the Earth. There are thousands of stories from people who **claim** that they have seen UFOs, met aliens or been on an alien planet. But **astronomers** and other scientists are more **sceptical**. They want facts not fiction. They say that the chances of meeting an alien are not very high and most of these stories come from people who have **visions**. Others have a lot of **imagination** and believe that what they imagined really happened.

Schau dir die markierten Wörter an und lies dazu folgende Tipps:

Vergleich: Was könnte das englische Wort *return* bedeuten? Überlege, ob du ein ähnliches Wort in einer anderen Sprache kennst: z.B das französische Wort *retourner*.
Logische Ableitung: Das Wort *body* ist dir bekannt. Was könnte dann *brain* sein, wenn es deinen Körper kontrolliert?
Kontext: Ein Wort wie *hideous* kannst du nur mithilfe der Wörter erraten, die es umgeben. Ist es wohl eher ein positives Wort wie *beautiful* oder ein negatives wie *horrible*?
Wortbildung: Du kennst bereits das Nomen *control*. Was könnte der Ausdruck *take control of* bedeuten? Das Verb *imagine* ist dir auch bekannt, so dass *imagination* leicht zu verstehen ist.
Deutsch: Die fehlenden drei neuen Wörter kannst du erraten, weil sie deutschen Wörtern ähneln: z.B.: *sceptical* = skeptisch.
Das heißt, du müsstest nur das Wort *claim* im Wörterbuch nachschlagen, falls du es doch nicht aus dem Kontext heraus verstehen kannst.

Nach dem zweiten Lesen:
1. Was ist das Hauptthema: Astronomers? The Earth? Aliens?
2. Wie ist die Argumentationskette bzw. der Handlungsverlauf: Welches sind die Argumente dafür und dagegen?/Was passiert?
3. Was ist die Schlussfolgerung?/Wie endet der Text?

Grammar summary | **Skills files** | Vocabulary

2 Texte verfassen

Anbei findest du acht Schritte *(steps)*, die dir helfen können einen guten Text zu schreiben.

1	Task	Was genau ist deine Aufgabe? Was für einen Text sollst du schreiben? Wozu? Worüber?
2	Content	Welche Punkte musst du erwähnen?
3	Type of text	Welche Merkmale hat ein solcher Text?
4	Plan	Mache einen Entwurf. Vergewissere dich, dass du keine Punkte vergessen hast.
5	Words and phrases	Welche *key words* gibt es zu dem Thema? Benutze ein Wörterbuch, falls du Hilfe brauchst. Fallen dir sogar schon ganze Sätze ein? Sammle alle Wörter, Halbsätze und Sätze in einer *mind map*.
6	First copy	Schreibe einen ersten Entwurf. Lass zwischen den Zeilen Platz frei, damit du Korrekturen einfügen kannst.
7	Partner check	Bitte einen Partner / eine Partnerin, deinen Text zu lesen. Versteht er / sie ihn? Baue seine / ihre Korrekturen in deinen Text mit ein.
8	Final copy	Schreibe den Text neu.

VORSICHT! Es gibt viele *false friends* und Fallen im Englischen. Das heißt, dass es manche gleich aussehende Wörter im Englischen und Deutschen gibt, die in den beiden Sprachen aber etwas anderes bedeuten. Hier sind ein paar Beispiele:

German	English	German	English
Handy	mobile (phone)	praktisch	handy
Gymnasium	grammar school	Turnhalle	gym(nasium)
Technik	technology	Methode	technique
Chips	crisps	Pommes frites	chips
Mappe	folder	Karte	map

The end of a beautiful friendship?

What's your handy number, Susan?

Handy number? What's that?

3 Eine Postkarte schreiben

Zwischen einer Postkarte aus dem englischsprachigen Ausland und einer Postkarte, wie du sie schreiben würdest, gibt es einige Unterschiede – und nicht nur sprachliche.

1	Greeting	*Hi*, oder *Hello*, mit Namen sind üblich. Du kannst auch *Dear* ... , sagen. Vergiss das Komma nach dem Namen nicht.
2	Date and place	Im *British English* schreibt man oft Datum und Ortsnamen oben rechts vom Text.
3	First word	Das erste Wort wird groß geschrieben.
4	About you	Sage, wie es dir geht und was du gerade tust. *(present continuous)*
5	The weather	Ein oder zwei kurze Sätze genügen.
6	A report	Sage, was du an welchem Tag gemacht hast. *(simple past)*
7	Future plans	Sage, was du vorhast *(want to, will, would like to, ...)* und wann.
8	Short forms	Es wird oft abgekürzt z. B. (*C U* ... , *Luv*)
9	Closing	Vergiss deinen Namen nicht. (*X* = ein Kuss, *O* = eine Umarmung)
10	The name	Anreden wie *Mr*, *Ms* oder *Mrs* brauchst du nicht in der Adresse.
11	The address	Schreibe die Adresse genauso auf, wie du sie von deinem Freund / deiner Freundin bekommen hast.
12	Postcode	Vergiss die Postleitzahl nicht. Sie steht **nach** dem Ort.
13	Country	Wenn du aus dem Ausland schreibst, gib das Zielland an.

6th August, Dublin **(2)**

Hi, Henry, **(1)**
(3) Just to say we are all well and we're having **(4)** a cool time in Ireland. The weather is great! It has been sunny since we arrived. **(5)** Yesterday we spent **(6)** the day in the zoo. Tomorrow **(7)** we want to go to the coast. We hope we can swim there. Hope **(8)** all is well with you and the family. See you **(8)** when we get back to Glasgow.

(8) Luv Fiona. XOX **(9)**

Henry McFarlane **(10)**

209 Westwind Street **(11)**

Glasgow

GL7 6YT **(12)**

Scotland **(13)**

Grammar summary | **Skills files**  | Vocabulary

4 Eine Bewerbung schreiben

Wenn du dich auf Englisch um eine Stelle bewirbst, solltest du neben einem Begleitbrief einen Lebenslauf (*CV*) und Kopien sämtlicher Zeugnisse mitschicken. Im Begleitbrief zeigst du, wie gut du schreiben und berichten kannst. Manchmal wird in der Anzeige ein handschriftlich geschriebener Brief verlangt. Übe, bevor du den Brief endgültig abschickst. Den Musterbrief unten kannst du als Vorlage verwenden.

Mr Richard Rich
Sunshine Film Studios
440 Brighton Road
London SW 6 9OP **(3)**

Suzie Tan **(1)**
239 Gordon Ave. **(2)**
Liverpool LI 56 7TU **(3)**

23 July 2012
Ref: Hol2397 **(5)**

Dear Mr Rich **(4)**

(6) With reference to your ad on the Internet on 20th July, I would like to apply for a job as a studio assistant at Sunshine Film Studios in London.
I finished school on June 26. At the moment I am working as an assistant for a photographer. It is a temporary position and I am looking for a permanent job. I would really like to work in London.
I looked at your company's homepage and some of your projects look very interesting. I have some experience of the film world. I had a holiday job in a TV studio last year. My special skills are organizing and working with people.
As you will see from my CV, I was born in China but I speak and write good English and German. I have some knowledge of Chinese, too. This could be useful with visitors who do not speak English.
I look forward to hearing from you soon.

Yours sincerely **(7)**
Suzie Tan

Encl. **(8)**

1	Name	In englischsprachigen Ländern schreibt man auch zuerst den Vornamen und dann den Nachnamen.
2	Address	Bei Adressen steht die Hausnummer vor dem Straßennamen. Abkürzungen wie *St.* (*Street*) , *Ave.* (*Avenue*), *Cl.* (*Close*), *Pde.* (*Parade*) sind üblich.
3	Postal codes	… sind unterschiedlich in verschiedenen Ländern. Falls du an eine Firma schreibst, schreibe die Adresse genau so, wie sie in der Anzeige steht.
4	Dear …,	Schreibe *Sir or Madam*, wenn du den Namen der Person nicht kennst. Bei Männernamen schreibe *Mr*, bei Frauennamen *Ms*.
5	Ref:	… bedeutet *reference* oder Betreff.
6	The first word	… schreibt man immer groß.
7	Closing	Wenn du die Anrede *Sir or Madam* verwendest, dann schreibst du *Yours faithfully*. Ansonsten *Yours sincerely*. Vergiss das „s" bei *Yours* nicht.
8	Encl.	= *enclosed* verwendest du, wenn du weitere Unterlagen beilegst (= Anlagen).

5 Einen Lebenslauf (CV) auf Englisch schreiben

Auf S. 74 siehst du einen teilweise ausgefüllten, englischen Lebenslauf (CV). **VORSICHT!** Es ist im englischsprachigen Raum nicht üblich, ein Foto mitzuschicken. Hier sind die wichtigsten Angaben:

1	Name	Vorname, dann Nachname
2	Address	mit Postleitzahl und Land
3	Tel.	mit internationaler Vorwahl
4	Email	Prüfe, ob du sie richtig geschrieben hast!
5	Date of birth	*British English* = Tag / Monat / Jahr *American English* = Monat / Tag / Jahr
6	Place of birth	Stadt + Land
7	Primary school	Voller Name und Adresse + Angabe der Jahreszahlen von … bis …
8	Secondary school	Voller Name und Adresse + Angabe der Jahreszahlen von … bis …
9	Examinations	Name und Datum der Prüfungen
10	Skills	Fähigkeiten und Fertigkeiten, die für den Job wichtig sind z. B.: *computer*, *photography*
11	Work experience	Praktika und Jobs, die du gemacht hast: Wo? Was? Wann?
12	Interests	Hobbys, Sport, ehrenamtliche Tätigkeiten usw.
13	Referees	Lehrer, Trainer, Arbeitgeber, … (Name, Adresse, Telefonnummer)

CV
CV (curriculum vitae) ist ein lateinischer Begriff und heißt übersetzt „course of life" (= Lebenslauf).

Referees
Falls der Arbeitgeber sich für dich interessiert, wird er sich mit deinen *referees* in Verbindung setzen. Du benötigst für deinen Arbeitgeber möglicherweise 2–3 Empfehlungsschreiben von *referees*. Sie sollten den Arbeitgeber über deine Persönlichkeit und deine Leistungen im Job informieren. (Bei Bewerbungen im englischsprachigen Raum bekommst du deine Empfehlungsbriefe nicht zu sehen.)

6 Eine formelle E-Mail schreiben

Wie bei einem formellen Brief, schreibst du in einer formellen E-Mail eine Anrede, eine Einleitung und ein paar abschließende Worte.

Der Betreff (*Re*) sagt, worum es geht.	*Re:*
Wenn du den Namen der angesprochenen Person nicht kennst, verwende die Form in Klammern.	*Dear (Sir or Madam) Mr / Ms … ,*
Das erste Wort wird groß geschrieben.	*With reference to your …*
Sei immer höflich, auch wenn du dich beschweren willst.	*Would it be possible to … ?* *I'd be very grateful if you could …* *I look forward to hearing from you.*
Verwende die richtige Schlussformel.	*Yours faithfully / sincerely* *…*

7 Einen englischen Geschäftsbrief schreiben

(1)   Swallows Garden Centres Ltd. • 75 Banbury Road • OXFORD • OX1 3JJ
      Tel: 01865 712257 • Email: info@swallows-gardencentres.co…uk
      www.swallows_gardencentres.co…uk

(2)   **Our ref: CM/jg**

(3)   23 March 20..

(4)   Otto Wolff GmbH
      An der Seilbahn 35
      42105 Wuppertal
      Germany

(5)   Dear Mr Skorikov

(6)   **Purchase order No. 1249**

(7)   Thank you for your offer of 21 March. Please find enclosed our purchase order.

We note that your prices include a 5% quantity discount for orders over 50 items and that the prices are DDP Oxford, England. We also note that for a first order you require payment in full with our order and we have today made a bank transfer to you of €14,962.50.

The consignment will be dispatched within 10 days of receipt of our payment.

(8)   Yours sincerely

(9)   *Charlotte Mitchell*

(10) Charlotte Mitchell
      Purchasing Manager

(11) Encl: Purchase order No. 1249

Gestaltung eines Geschäftsbriefs
Es gibt keine standardmäßige Gestaltung für einen englischen Geschäftsbrief. Gängig ist die Gestaltung, die hier verwendet wird, bei der nach dem Briefkopf alle Zeilen linksbündig sind.

1 **Letterhead** *(Briefkopf)*
Im Briefkopf stehen Firmenname, Postadresse und andere Kontaktdaten wie Telefonnummer und Internetadresse. Oft wird hier ein Firmenlogo abgedruckt.

2 **Reference(s)** *(Zeichen)*
Die Zeichen beinhalten die Initialen der Person, die den Brief verfasst hat (hier C̲harlotte M̲itchell), und der Person, die den Brief getippt hat (hier J̲enny G̲off). Im Antwortschreiben gibt man diese Zeichen an und schreibt: 'Your ref.'

3 **Date** *(Datum)*
Um Missverständnisse zu vermeiden, sollte das Datum immer ausgeschrieben werden – 09.10. ist in den USA der 10. September, in Europa dagegen der 9. Oktober.

4 **Inside address** *(Empfängeranschrift)*
Das ist die Empfängeranschrift. Wenn man an eine Adresse im Vereinigten Königreich schreibt, sollte man das Postleitzahl in eine extra Zeile unter den Namen der Stadt schreiben. Außerdem sollte man nicht vergessen, dass in britischen und amerikanischen Adressen die Hausnummer vor dem Straßennamen steht. (75 Banbury Road).

5/8 **Salutation / Complimentary close** *(Anrede / Schlussformel)*
Anrede und Schlussformel sind miteinander verbunden: Welche Schlussformel (8) in einem Brief verwendet wird, hängt davon ab, welche Anrede (5) zu Beginn des Briefes verwendet wurde. Wenn man eine Firma zum ersten Mal anschreibt und den Namen des Ansprechpartners nicht kennt, beginnt man mit *Dear Sirs* oder *Dear Sir or Madam* und beendet den Brief mit *Yours faithfully*. Später, wenn man den Namen weiß, schreibt man *Dear (Mr … / Mrs … / Ms …)* und beendet den Brief weniger formell mit *Yours sincerely*. Wenn man einen Geschäftspartner wirklich gut kennt, kann man auch mit *Dear (Vorname)* beginnen und mit einer freundlichen Schlussformel enden, wie *Kind regards* oder *Best wishes*.

6 **Subject line** *(Betreffzeile)*
Die Betreffzeile wird in **fetten** Buchstaben geschrieben oder unterstrichen. Sie steht nach der Anrede.

7 **Body of the letter** *(Hauptteil des Briefes)*
Das erste Wort des Hauptteils des Briefes fängt immer mit einen GROẞBUCHSTABEN an. Absätze werden durch Leerzeilen getrennt.

9/10 **Signature** *(Unterschrift)*
Die Person, die den Brief verfasst, unterschreibt den Brief handschriftlich. Da Unterschriften aber oft schwer zu lesen sind, wird der Name der unterschreibenden Person nochmals unter der Unterschrift abgedruckt, oft zusammen mit der Funktion dieser Person in der Firma.

11 **Enclosure(s)** *(Anlagen)*
'Enclosures' sind Dokumente oder andere Dinge, die dem Brief beigelegt werden (hier ein Bestellformular).

Grammar summary | **Skills files** | Vocabulary

8 Hörtexte verstehen

Vor dem Hören:
Es hilft dir, folgende Punkte zu klären, bevor du versuchst, einen Hörtext zu verstehen:

1. Kontext: Wo kommt der Text her? Was weißt du schon über solche Texte?

Medien			Öffentliche Ansagen			Persönliche Gespräche im Alltag		
Radio	TV	…	Bahnhof	Flughafen	…	live	Telefon	…
Hörspiel, Interview, Film			Z. B. Ansage			Anruf, Gespräch, …		
Oft handelt es sich um einen Bericht oder ein Interview.			Die gesuchte Info kann mit einem Schlüsselwort herausgehört werden. Der Rest ist unwichtig.			Du kannst immer nachfragen, wenn du etwas nicht verstanden hast.		

2. Vorwissen: Was kann dir sonst noch beim Erschließen helfen?

Der Titel	Ein Bild	Die Einführung	Sonstige Kenntnisse
… kann bei einem Film oder einer Sendung hilfreich sein.	… hilft oft dabei, sich ein Bild vom Sprecher bzw. von einer anderen Person/Personen zu machen.	… gibt Hintergrundinformationen bzw. erklärt die Situation.	Wie ist die Person, mit der du redest? Wie könnte sie reagieren?

3. Was möchtest du von dem Text erfahren? (Wer? Wann? Was? Wie? Wo? Warum?)

Allgemeines	Bestimmte Details	Eine Information
Was ist das Hauptthema? Um welches Problem/welchen Inhalt geht es?	Wer redet? Welche Angaben werden zu einem Problem/Thema gemacht?	Detaillierte Angaben zu einer bestimmten Frage, z. B. „Wann fährt der nächste Zug?"

Während des Hörens:
Mach dir Notizen.
1. Falls du dir mehrere Punkte notieren willst, kannst du eine Liste, eine *mind map* oder eine Tabelle anfertigen.
2. Hör dir den Text bei einer Prüfung zwei- oder dreimal an. Im Alltag ist das nicht möglich, aber dann kannst du immer jemanden fragen.
3. Prüfe, ob du alle Infos hast, die du brauchst.

Nach dem Hören:
Erledige sämtliche Aufgaben mithilfe deiner Notizen. Falls du mit einem Partner/einer Partnerin zusammenarbeitest, vergleicht eure Ergebnisse.

9 Sich auf ein Vorstellungsgespräch vorbereiten

Es ist sehr wichtig, sich auf das Gespräch gut vorzubereiten. Dann kannst du dich während des Vorstellungsgesprächs besser auf das Wesentliche konzentrieren.

Before the interview	1. Informiere dich über die Stelle / das Land / die Firma / … 2. Überlege dir 2–3 Fragen, die du stellen kannst. 3. Mach dir Gedanken, was du zu dem Vorstellungsgespräch anziehst: einen Anzug / Rock / eine Jeans? Deine Kleidung muss auf jeden Fall sauber und gepflegt sein. Trage nicht zu viel Schmuck / Make-up. 4. Bereite dich darauf vor, Fragen des Interviewers zu beantworten.
During the interview	1. Versuche dich zu entspannen. Schau den Interviewer an und lächle! Gib ihm / ihr die Hand, wenn er / sie es möchte. Deine ersten Worte sind wichtig. 2. Achte darauf, wie der Interviewer mit dir redet: Formell? Freundlich? 3. Mach dir keine Sorgen, wenn du nicht alles verstehst. Der Interviewer weiß, dass dein Englisch nicht perfekt ist. Sei ehrlich!

You can ask on the phone	*What do I need to bring with me?* *(Do you pay travel costs?)*	
The interviewer could say	Formal: *Good morning / afternoon / …,* *Mr / Ms …* *Nice to meet you.* *Please take a seat / sit down,* *Mr / Ms …*	Informal: *Hi / Hello, Pete / Sue / … !* *Take a seat!*
The interviewer could ask	*Why are you interested in this job?* *Have you worked abroad before?* *What are your best subjects?* *What would you do if you had a difficult customer? / …* *Do you have any questions?*	
If you don't understand something, you can ask	*Could you repeat the question, please?* *Excuse me. Could you say that again, please?* *Excuse me. What does (the word) … mean?* *I'm sorry. Could you speak more slowly, please?*	
You can ask at the interview	*How big is your company?* *How many people work here?*	

Grammar summary | **Skills files** | Vocabulary

10 Ein Interview mit jemandem führen

Bevor du ein Interview führst, ist es wichtig, dass du versuchst im Voraus etwas über die Person bzw. das Thema zu erfahren. So kannst du leichter Fragen stellen. Das Interview wird dadurch interessanter.

Tipps	Im Studio	Auf der Straße
1. Be polite.	Good morning / afternoon … My name is / I'm … Thank you for coming to the studio / …	Excuse me. I'm from … School. May I ask you a question about / your opinion on …?
2. Prepare your questions.		
Beginne mit einem Fragewort.	**Who** do you …? / **What** have you …? / **Why** did you …?	**What** is your opinion on …?
Beginne mit einem Verb.	**Can** you tell me …? / **Have** you ever …? / **Is** it true that …?	**Do** you think people should …? **Can** you remember …?
Beginne mit einer höflichen Einladung / Aufforderung.	**Please, tell** us about … / **explain** …	**Could you** say something about …? **Would you** be prepared to give us your opinion on …?
3. Say goodbye.		
Bedanke dich und sage noch etwas Nettes.	**Thank you** very much … That was very interesting / … **We hope** you enjoy your stay in …	**Thank you** Sir / Madam / … You have been very helpful. **Have a nice day.**

11 Eine Präsentation vorbereiten

1. Schreibt zunächst ein Handout und macht Kopien für die Klasse. Hier ein Beispiel:

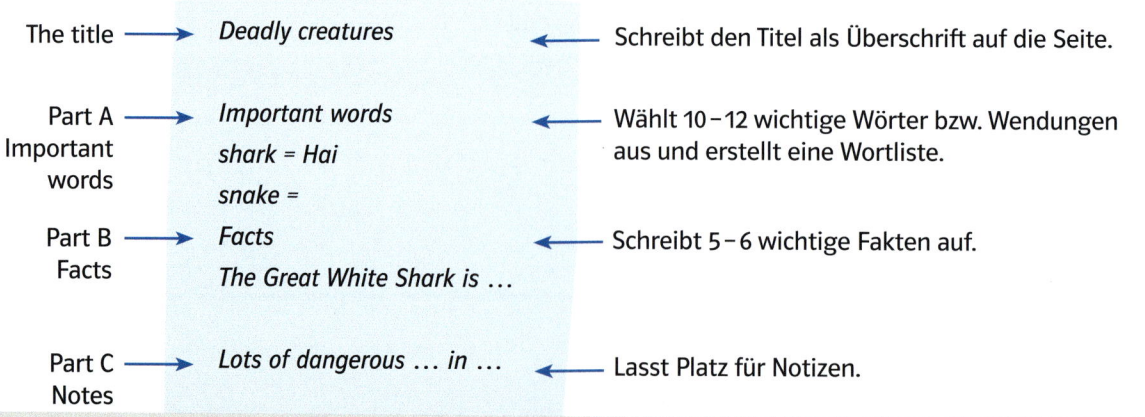

The title → *Deadly creatures* ← Schreibt den Titel als Überschrift auf die Seite.

Part A Important words → *Important words* *shark = Hai* *snake =* ← Wählt 10–12 wichtige Wörter bzw. Wendungen aus und erstellt eine Wortliste.

Part B Facts → *Facts* *The Great White Shark is …* ← Schreibt 5–6 wichtige Fakten auf.

Part C Notes → *Lots of dangerous … in …* ← Lasst Platz für Notizen.

2. Wählt eine Präsentationsform, die ihr interessant findet und bei der ihr eure Talente am besten anwenden könnt. Hier ein paar Beispiele:

| **A display** (talents: drawing, designing) | **A demonstration** (talents: making / explaining things) | **A sales talk** (talents: public speaking) |
| **A discussion** (talents: speaking, working in a group) | **A performance** (talents: singing, performing, acting) | **A computer presentation** (talents: using equipment, typing) |

Weitere Präsentationsformen, die ihr in diesem Buch findet, sind:
a web page, an advert, an interview, a talk show, a PowerPoint presentation, a reading, a quiz, a summary, a report, a talk, a gallery walk.

3. Tipps für eine PowerPoint-Präsentation:

Tipps

1. Plan your presentation on paper first.
2. Write down a title.
3. Write down the aspects of the topic as a list.
4. Write a few key words on each aspect.
5. Start your PowerPoint programme.
6. Type the title on to one 'page' and your key words on to the other 'pages'. Use your key words in sentences during your presentation.
7. Use pictures and diagrams to improve your presentation.

4. Überprüft, ob eure Mitschüler/innen alles verstanden haben, was ihr ihnen gezeigt bzw. erzählt habt.

A written test	Das können z. B. Fragen, ein Lückentext, ein beschriftetes Diagramm, ein Quiz, ein Kreuzworträtsel, ein Fehlertext bzw. ein Fehlerbild sein.
An oral test	Spiele aller Art: Rollenspiele, Ratespiele, Nacherzählungen, Interviews, Zusammenfassungen, … , z. B.: Ein Kartenspiel: Schreibe Fragen auf Kärtchen. Die anderen ziehen eine Karte und beantworten die Frage.

12 Eine Diskussion / Debatte durchführen

Es gibt viele verschiedene Arten einer Diskussion / Debatte. Folgende Tipps und Redewendungen können euch helfen:

	Tipps	Ausdrücke
1	Einigt euch auf eine Aussage (*statement / motion*).	*I think … is a good statement.* *I'd like to suggest … as our statement.* *Let's vote on it. Who's for / against the statement …*
2	Schreibt sie an die Tafel.	*Statement: Everybody should work for a short time in another country.*
3	Wer macht den Vorsitz? Er / Sie muss die Diskussion / Debatte mithilfe der Sätze rechts leiten.	*Good morning / afternoon.* *Our statement for today's discussion is: …* *Speakers for / against the statement are …* *The first speaker for / against the statement is …* *… , it's your turn. You may speak now.* *Thank you … . Your time is up.*
4	Die Sprecher sammeln Argumente für und gegen die Aussage.	*I agree / don't agree with the statement.* *In my opinion …* *I think it is wrong / important to say that …*
5	Der / Die Vorsitzende fragt, ob andere ihre Meinung äußern möchten.	*Yes, … , what would you like to say?*
6	Der / Die Vorsitzende beendet die Diskussion / Debatte und fordert zur Abstimmung auf.	*Please raise your hand if you are for / against the statement.* *The results of the vote are … for and … against the statement.*

13 Think-Pair-Share (T-P-S)

Du liest und hörst in der Klasse oft: *Compare your answers with a partner, then report to the class.* Dies wird *Think-Pair-Share* genannt. So funktioniert es:
- Mach dir Gedanken zu der Aufgabe und notiere sie. Dein Lehrer kann dir eine zeitliche Grenze von z. B. 5 Minuten geben.
- Finde eine/n Partner/in. Lest euch eure Notizen gegenseitig vor. Zeig sie deinem/r Partner/in nicht! Dies ist eine Sprechaktivität.
- Korrigiert eure Notizen, wenn ihr einen Fehler findet oder fügt neue Informationen hinzu, wenn eine/r von euch eine bessere Idee hat.
- Du oder dein/e Partner/in präsentiert eure gemeinsamen Ideen der Klasse, oder wenn die Aufgabe lang genug ist, stellt ihr sie beide abwechselnd vor.

14 Cheat sheet

Cheat sheet heißt auf Deutsch *Spickzettel* und ist eine gute Möglichkeit, einen Text zusammenzufassen und eine kurze Präsentation darüber zu halten. So funktioniert es:
- Geh den Text durch und notiere Schlüsselbegriffe und wichtige Ausdrücke auf ein kleines Stück Papier. Diese Schlüsselbegriffe enthalten die wichtigsten Informationen des Textes.
- Gehe deine Notizen durch und streiche alle Wörter durch, die nicht absolut notwendig sind! Idealerweise solltest du nur einen Schlüsselbegriff für jeden Teil des Textes haben.
- Verwende deine Liste *(cheat sheet)*, um deine Präsentation zu halten. Die Schlüsselbegriffe helfen dir, dir zu merken, was du sagen willst, aber du solltest soweit wie möglich deine eigenen Worte benutzen. Wiederhole nicht einfach den Originaltext!

15 Gallery walk

Am Ende vieler Gruppenarbeiten in der Klasse werdet ihr einen Text, z. B. eine E-Mail oder vielleicht ein Poster produziert haben. Ein *gallery walk* ist eine Möglichkeit, eure Arbeitsergebnisse in der Klasse zu zeigen. So funktioniert es:
- Hängt die Ergebnisse aller Gruppen im Klassenraum auf und verteilt sie soweit voneinander entfernt wie möglich.
- Dann schaut ihr euch jede Gruppenarbeit im Klassenzimmer an.
- Wenn du bei deiner Arbeit angekommen bist, halte dort an und sei bereit, sie zu erklären und Fragen der Klasse hierzu zu beantworten. Jede/r in deiner Gruppe sollte hierzu in der Lage sein.
- Fahrt in dieser Weise fort, bis jede/r alle Arbeiten gesehen hat.
- Zum Schluss diskutiert ihr die Ergebnisse in der Klasse. Welches war das beliebteste / interessanteste / am besten präsentierte? Warum?

| Grammar summary | Skills files | Vocabulary

Unitbegleitendes Vokabular

Videotraining: Englische Aussprache

Perfekte englische Aussprache leicht gemacht: Mit dem Lernprogramm zur englischen Lautschrift können Sie alle Laute einüben. Wählen Sie einfach in der Navigation rechts den entsprechenden Reiter (*Vowels* oder *Consonants*) aus und klicken Sie dann auf das gewünschte phonetische Symbol. Sprechen Sie die Wörter laut nach.

Unter www.klett.de geben Sie bitte den Code unter der Abbildung rechts ein.

n633sn

Abkürzungen und Zeichen

etw	= etwa	L	= links	1A	Vor den Vokabeln findest du immer die jeweiligen Übungsnummern der Unit.
pl	= Plural, Mehrzahl	R	= rechts		
sb	= somebody				
sth	= something	=	entspricht		
BE	= britisches Englisch	↔	ist das Gegenteil von	**blue**	Vokabel aus Hörtext
AE	= amerikanisches Englisch	→	verwandt mit		
AustrE	= australisches Englisch	!	Achtung		
NewZE	= neuseeländisches Englisch				

Unit 1 Get ready for work!

	to get ready (got, got) [ˌget ˈredi]	sich bereitmachen	I must get ready for the party tonight.
1A	opposite [ˈɒpəzɪt]	gegenüber	That girl that lives in the house opposite mine.
	notes [nəʊts]	Notizen	
	background [ˈbækɡraʊnd]	Hintergrund	The man in the background has a red shirt.
2A	all day [ˌɔːl ˈdeɪ]	den ganzen Tag lang	
	at lunchtime [ət ˈlʌntʃtaɪm]	mittags	At lunchtime we always go out for a sandwich.
	That depends. [ðət dɪˈpendz]	Das kommt darauf an.	
	kind [kaɪnd]	Art, Sorte	It tastes sweet – it's a kind of fruit.
	beginning [bɪˈɡɪnɪŋ]	Anfang	
	hairdressing [ˈheədresɪŋ]	Friseur-, Friseurhandwerk	hairdressing → hairdresser
	trainee [treɪˈniː]	Auszubildende/r	trainee → trainer → to train
	woodworking [ˈwʊdwɜːkɪŋ]	Holzbe-/-verarbeitung, Holz-	
	to train to be sb [ˌtreɪn tə ˈbi]	eine Ausbildung zum / zur … machen	He wants to train to be a pilot.
	carpenter [ˈkɑːpəntə]	Zimmermann, Schreiner	
	wood [wʊd]	Holz	
2B	sense [sens]	Sinn	
	humour [ˈhjuːmə]	Humor	She's always laughing. She has a great sense of humour.
	maths [mæθs]	Mathe(matik)	
	fantastic [fænˈtæstɪk]	großartig, fantastisch	

	to expect [ɪkˈspekt]	erwarten	
	to expect sb to do sth [ɪkˈspekt]	von jdm erwarten, etw zu tun	They expect me to be there at 9 o'clock every day.
	on one's own [ɒn wʌnz ˈəʊn]	allein	
	self-discipline [ˌself ˈdɪsəplɪn]	Selbstdisziplin	Sue never gets angry. She has a lot of self-discipline.
	adult [ˈædʌlt]	Erwachsene/r	! Betonung
	industry [ˈɪndəstri]	Branche, Industrie	industry → industrial
2C	result [rɪˈzʌlt]	Ergebnis	
	chart [tʃɑːt]	Tabelle, Diagramm	
3A	nursery [ˈnɜːsəri]	Kindertagesstätte	
	nursery worker [ˈnɜːsəri wɜːkə]	Kindergärtner/in, Erzieher/in	
	to feed [fiːd]	füttern	You feed animals and babies.
	to change a baby [ˌtʃeɪndʒ ə ˈbeɪbi]	einem Baby die Windeln wechseln	
	to make sure [ˌmeɪk ˈʃʊə]	sicherstellen, gewährleisten	Can you make sure the light is out, please.
	safe [seɪf]	sicher	
	safety [ˈseɪfti]	Sicherheit	These days cars have many safety features.
	responsible [rɪˈspɒnsəbl]	verantwortungsbewusst	
	caring [ˈkeərɪŋ]	fürsorglich	Nursing is a caring profession.
	administrative assistant [ədˌmɪnɪstrətɪv əˈsɪstənt]	Verwaltungsassistent/in	
	day-to-day [ˌdeɪ tə ˈdeɪ]	tagesaktuell, alltäglich	
	smoothly [ˈsmuːðli]	reibungslos, glatt	It's important that it goes smoothly and the guests are happy.
	telephone [ˈtelɪfəʊn]	Telefon	
	to type [taɪp]	tippen	Where did you learn to type so fast?
	to photocopy [ˈfəʊtəʊkɒpi]	fotokopieren	
	to print [prɪnt]	drucken, ausdrucken	
	accurate [ˈækjərət]	genau	accurate ↔ inaccurate
	to communicate [kəˈmjuːnɪkeɪt]	kommunizieren	to communicate → communication
4A	bracket [ˈbrækɪt]	Klammer	
4F	clever [ˈklevə]	intelligent, gescheit	! Nicht das Deutsche clever
	creative [kriˈeɪtɪv]	kreativ, schöpferisch	creative → creation → to create
	prize [praɪz]	Preis, Auszeichnung	
4G	hometown [ˌhəʊmˈtaʊn]	Heimatstadt	
	class trip [ˈklɑːs trɪp]	Klassenfahrt	
	chips [tʃɪps]	(BE:) Pommes frites	! Crisps = Kartoffelchips
4H	sick [sɪk]	krank	He was so sick he couldn't go to school.
	nurse [nɜːs]	Krankenschwester, Krankenpfleger	
	one day [ˌwʌn ˈdeɪ]	(irgendwann) einmal	One day he wants to climb Mount Everest.
	to paint [peɪnt]	malen	
	to decorate [ˈdekəreɪt]	tapezieren	to decorate → decoration
	flat [flæt]	(BE:) Wohnung	
	No smoking. [ˌnəʊ ˈsməʊkɪŋ]	Rauchen verboten.	
5A	link [lɪŋk]	Verbindung, Kontakt	
	based on [ˈbeɪst ɒn]	anhand von, basierend auf	The film is based on a true story.
	conference [ˈkɒnfərəns]	Konferenz	
	to introduce sb [ˌɪntrəˈdjuːs]	jdn vorstellen	I'd like to introduce you to my parents.
	talk [tɔːk]	Vortrag	
	to give a talk [ˌgɪv ə ˈtɔːk]	einen Vortrag halten	
	daily routine [ˌdeɪli ruːˈtiːn]	(routinemäßiger) Tagesablauf	
V	careers advice centre [kəˈrɪəz ədvaɪs sentə]	Berufsberatung(szentrum)	
	dream [driːm]	Traum	a dream about sth

| Grammar summary | Skills files | **Vocabulary** |

Unit 2 Travelling for work

1A	tram [træm]	Straßenbahn, Tram	
	hardly ever [ˌhɑːdli 'evə]	kaum (jemals)	I hardly ever see you any more.
1B	business trip ['bɪznəs trɪp]	Geschäftsreise	
	to check in [ˌtʃek 'ɪn]	einchecken	When she arrived, she checked in at the hotel.
	check-in ['tʃekɪn]	Abfertigung	
	check-in desk ['tʃekɪn desk]	Abfertigungsschalter	
	clerk [klɑːk]	Angestellte/r	
	boarding card ['bɔːdɪŋ kɑːd]	Bordkarte	To board is to get on a plane or a ship.
1C	machine [məˈʃiːn]	Gerät, Maschine	
2A	passenger ['pæsɪndʒə]	Passagier	
	departure [dɪˈpɑːtʃə]	Abflug, Abfahrt	Abkürzung = dep.
	departures [dɪˈpɑːtʃəz]	Abflughalle, Terminal	
	gate [ɡeɪt]	Flugsteig, Gate	
	to depart [dɪˈpɑːt]	abfliegen, abfahren	to depart ↔ to arrive
	security check [sɪˈkjʊərəti tʃek]	Sicherheitskontrolle	
	security officer [sɪˈkjʊərəti ɒfɪsə]	Sicherheitsbeamte/r, -beauftragte/r	
	baggage ['bæɡɪdʒ]	Gepäck	! Baggage ist Singular: The baggage is …
	through [θruː]	durch (… hindurch)	! Aussprache: -ough wie –o in do
	passport ['pɑːspɔːt]	Pass, Reisepass	You need a passport to leave the country.
	passport check ['pɑːspɔːt tʃek]	Passkontrolle	
	passport officer ['pɑːspɔːt ɒfɪsə]	Passbeamte/r	
	to board [bɔːd]	an Bord gehen	
	baggage reclaim [ˌbæɡɪdʒ 'riːkleɪm]	Gepäckausgabe	
	customs ['kʌstəmz]	Zoll	The customs allow you to bring in one bottle of wine.
	customs check ['kʌstəmz tʃek]	Zollkontrolle	
	customs officer ['kʌstəmz ɒfɪsə]	Zollbeamter	
	seat [siːt]	Sitz	I want a seat by the window.
2B	heading ['hedɪŋ]	Überschrift	
	arrival [əˈraɪvl]	Ankunft	
2C	definition [ˌdefɪˈnɪʃn]	Definition	
2E	pilot ['paɪlət]	Pilot/in	
3A	exciting [ɪkˈsaɪtɪŋ]	aufregend, spannend	! an exciting film; an excited child
	roller coaster ['rəʊlə kəʊstə]	Achterbahn	
	theme park ['θiːm pɑːk]	Vergnügungs-, Themenpark	Theme parks are popular with children.
	fair [feə]	Jahrmarkt	
	electrical technician [ɪˌlektrɪkl tekˈnɪʃn]	Elektriker/in	
	equipment [ɪˈkwɪpmənt]	Geräte, Ausrüstung, Ausstattung	The equipment they have is very old.
	to service ['sɜːvɪs]	warten, instandhalten	
	on foot [ɒn 'fʊt]	zu Fuß	! on foot; by bus, by train, by boat, by plane
	ideal [aɪˈdiːəl]	ideal	
	playground ['pleɪɡraʊnd]	Spielplatz	
	children's playground [ˌtʃɪldrənz 'pleɪɡraʊnd]	Kinderspielplatz	
	Wi-Fi ['waɪ faɪ]	drahtlos, wireless	
	connection [kəˈnekʃn]	Verbindung	connection → to connect
	to note sth [nəʊt]	(etw) beachten	
	non-smoking [ˌnɒnˈsməʊkɪŋ]	Nichtraucher-	
	total ['təʊtl]	Gesamtanzahl	If you add 3 and 6, it comes to a total of 9.
3B	key [kiː]	Schlüssel	
	registration [ˌredʒɪˈstreɪʃn]	Anmeldung	registration → to register
	registration form [ˌredʒɪˈstreɪʃn fɔːm]	Formular	
	to fill in [ˌfɪl 'ɪn]	ausfüllen	Fill this in, sign it and give it to me.

	to enjoy sth [ɪnˈdʒɔɪ]	etw genießen	
	stay [steɪ]	Aufenthalt	stay → to stay
4A	in full [ɪn ˈfʊl]	vollständig	
4B	finally [ˈfaɪnəli]	schließlich, endlich	Tired and hungry, we finally arrived.
4C	to include [ɪnˈkluːd]	einbeziehen, einschließen	
4D	alcoholic [ˌælkəˈhɒlɪk]	alkoholisch	alcoholic → alcohol
5A	postcard [ˈpəʊstkɑːd]	Postkarte	
	Best wishes, [ˌbest ˈwɪʃɪz]	(Brief:) Alles Gute	
5B	role-play [ˈrəʊl pleɪ]	Rollenspiel	
	to role-play [ˈrəʊl pleɪ]	in einem Rollenspiel darstellen	
	part [pɑːt]	Rolle	

Unit 3 A visit to a company

1A	apprentice [əˈprentɪs]	Auszubildende/r, Lehrling	apprentice → apprenticeship
	chemicals [ˈkemɪklz]	Chemikalien	
	chemicals company [ˈkemɪklz kʌmpəni]	Chemiebetrieb	
	laboratory [ləˈbɒrətri]	Labor	! Betonung
	trainer [ˈtreɪnə]	Ausbilder/in	
	paint [peɪnt]	Farbe	paint → to paint
	PLC [ˌpiː el ˈsiː]	AG, Aktiengesellschaft	= Public Limited Co.
	a couple of [ə ˈkʌpl əv]	ein paar	Wait a moment. There are a couple of things I need to do.
1B	quite [kwaɪt]	ziemlich, recht	It is quite hot today, nearly 25°.
	satisfactorily [ˌsætɪsˈfæktərəli]	zufriedenstellend	
	badly [ˈbædli]	schlecht	badly ↔ well
2A	to grow (grew, grown) [grəʊ]	wachsen	Bamboo is a plant which grows very fast.
	manufacturer [ˌmænjuˈfæktʃərə]	Hersteller, Fabrikant	manufacturer ↔ to manufacture
	head office [ˌhed ˈɒfɪs]	Zentrale	
	Russia [ˈrʌʃə]	Russland	Russia → Russian
	process [ˈprəʊses]	Prozess, Vorgang, Verfahren	
	automatically [ˌɔːtəˈmætɪkli]	automatisch	The light goes on automatically when you enter the room.
	robot [ˈrəʊbɒt]	Roboter	
	home [həʊm]	Haus, Wohnung, Zuhause	He works in London, but his home is in Manchester.
	building [ˈbɪldɪŋ]	Gebäude	
	tractor [ˈtræktə]	Traktor	Farmers drive tractors.
	bridge [brɪdʒ]	Brücke	The bridge goes over the river.
	DIY (Do-it-yourself) [ˌdiː aɪ ˈwaɪ]	Heimwerken	
	DIY shop [ˌdiː aɪ ˈwaɪ ʃɒp]	Baumarkt	
	exactly [ɪgˈzæktli]	genau	It is now exactly 9:14.
	to be happy [bi ˈhæpi]	sich freuen	to be happy ↔ to be sad
2B	automatic [ˌɔːtəˈmætɪk]	automatisch	
2C	exact [ɪgˈzækt]	genau	Nobody knows the exact numbers.
	Nice to meet you. [ˌnaɪs tə ˈmiːt ju]	Schön, Sie kennenzulernen.	
	Pleased to meet you. [ˌpliːzd tə ˈmiːt ju]	Schön, Sie kennenzulernen. Sehr angenehm.	
	to look round [ˌlʊk ˈraʊnd]	sich umsehen	Would you like to look round the house?
	this way [ˈðɪs weɪ]	hier entlang	
2D	to act [ækt]	spielen, schauspielern	to act → actor → actress
3A	tour [tʊə]	Rundgang, Tour	There's a tour of the town every day.
	raw materials [ˌrɔː məˈtɪəriəlz]	Rohstoffe	
	production [prəˈdʌkʃn]	Produktion	production → to produce → product
	quality [ˈkwɒləti]	Qualität	
	quality control [ˈkwɒləti kəntrəʊl]	Qualitätskontrolle	

	warehouse ['weəhaʊs]	Lager	
	entrance ['entrəns]	Eingang	entrance ↔ exit
	dispatch [dɪ'spætʃ]	Versand	
3B	powder ['paʊdə]	Pulver	You wash clothes with washing powder.
	oil [ɔɪl]	Öl	
	to store [stɔː]	lagern, speichern	If you store something, you keep it and use it later.
	tank [tæŋk]	Tank	
	up there [ʌp 'ðeə]	da oben	up there ↔ down there
	to mix [mɪks]	mischen	Mix the egg and the milk.
	at the moment [ət ðə 'məʊmənt]	im Augenblick	= now
	can [kæn]	Dose	
	to load [ləʊd]	laden, verladen	to load ↔ to unload
	onto ['ɒntə]	auf	
	research and development [rɪˌsɜːtʃ ən dɪ'veləpmənt]	Forschungs- und Entwicklungsabteilung	Abkürzung: R & D
	administrative [əd'mɪnɪstrətɪv]	Verwaltungs-	administrative → to administer → administration
4A	to open ['əʊpən]	sich öffnen	These doors open automatically.
	report [rɪ'pɔːt]	Bericht	
4B	because of [bɪ'kɒz əv]	aufgrund von, wegen	We didn't leave on time because of the snow.
	match [mætʃ]	Spiel, Partie	
4C	expression [ɪk'spreʃn]	Ausdruck	Good luck! is an expression you often hear.
4E	electronic [ˌɪlek'trɒnɪk]	elektronisch	
	to dispatch [dɪ'spætʃ]	versenden	= to send
5A	(the) following ['fɒləʊɪŋ]	der/die/das folgende	
5B	Japan [dʒə'pæn]	Japan	Japan → Japanese
5A	location [ləʊ'keɪʃn]	Ort, Standort	They bought a house in a good location.
V	schedule ['ʃedjuːl]	(Termin-)Plan	I'm very busy. I have a full schedule.
	facility [fə'sɪləti]	Anlage, Einrichtung	
	test facility ['test fəsɪləti]	Versuchseinrichtung, Testanlage	
	test manager ['test mænɪdʒə]	Versuchsleiter/in	
	managing director [ˌmænɪdʒɪŋ də'rektə]	Geschäftsführer/in	
	factory manager ['fæktəri mænɪdʒə]	Betriebsleiter/in, Werksleiter/in	

Unit 4 Global business

1	global ['gləʊbl]	weltumspannend, global	
1A	delivery [dɪ'lɪvəri]	Lieferung	delivery → to deliver
	bakery ['beɪkəri]	Bäckerei	bakery → to bake
1B	cheese [tʃiːz]	Käse	
	pepperoni [pepə'rəʊni]	Peperoni	
	sausage ['sɒsɪdʒ]	Wurst	
	chocolate ['tʃɒklət]	Schokolade	! chocolates = Pralinen
	marmalade ['mɑːməleɪd]	Marmelade	Marmalade is always made with bitter oranges.
	Asia ['eɪʃə]	Asien	Asia → Asian
	Italy ['ɪtəli]	Italien	Italy → Italian
	label ['leɪbl]	Etikett	The label says it's made in Italy.
2B	mouse, mice [maʊs, maɪs]	Maus, Mäuse	
	keyboard ['kiːbɔːd]	Tastatur	
	to manufacture [ˌmænju'fæktʃə]	herstellen	
	tower ['taʊə]	Turm	
	hard drive [ˌhɑːd 'draɪv]	Festplatte	
	motherboard ['mʌðəbɔːd]	Hauptplatine	
	CPU [ˌsiː piː 'juː]	CPU	
	central ['sentrəl]	zentral	Central heating keeps the whole house warm.
	to process ['prəʊses]	verarbeiten	

	unit ['juːnɪt]	Einheit	They sell 10,000 units a year.
	to assemble [əˈsembl]	montieren, zusammenbauen	
2C	**Ireland** [ˈaɪələnd]	Irland	Ireland → Irish
	assembly [əˈsembli]	Montage	
	Czech Republic [ˌtʃek rɪˈpʌblɪk]	Tschechische Republik	
	Singapore [ˌsɪŋəˈpɔː]	Singapur	
3A	**globalisation** [ˌɡləʊbəlaɪˈzeɪʃn]	Globalisierung	
	Kenya [ˈkenjə]	Kenia	
	farm [fɑːm]	Farm, Bauernhof	farm → to farm
	to grow (grew, grown) [ɡrəʊ]	(Pflanze:) anbauen	You can't grow oranges in Scotland.
	farmer [ˈfɑːmə]	Farmer/in, Bauer/Bäuerin	
	grower [ˈɡrəʊə]	Bauer/Bäuerin, Pflanzer/in	
	tourism [ˈtʊərɪzəm]	Tourismus	Tourism is a big business in Spain.
	to be on sale [bi ˌɒn ˈseɪl]	erhältlich sein, zum Verkauf stehen	The new model has been on sale since Monday.
	market [ˈmɑːkɪt]	Markt	
	to import [ɪmˈpɔːt]	importieren	to import ↔ to export
	Silicon Valley [ˌsɪlɪkən ˈvæli]	Computerzentrum in Kalifornien	
	India [ˈɪndiə]	Indien	
	on the telephone [ɒn ðə ˈtelɪfəʊn]	am Telefon	on the computer – on the internet – on the radio – on the television
	helpline [ˈhelplaɪn]	Hotline	
	salary [ˈsæləri]	Gehalt	
	euro [ˈjʊərəʊ]	Euro	
	poor [pʊə]	arm	poor ↔ rich
	mine [maɪn]	Bergwerk	
	cheaply [ˈtʃiːpli]	billig	You can buy things cheaply at markets.
3C	**on the one hand** [ɒn ðə ˈwʌn hænd]	einerseits	
	on the other hand [ɒn ði ˈʌðə hænd]	andererseits	
4B	**vase** [vɑːz]	Vase	a vase of flowers
	by sea [baɪ ˈsiː]	auf dem Seeweg	I travelled by sea and by land.
	tonne [tʌn]	Tonne	
	catastrophe [kəˈtæstrəfi]	Katastrophe	! Betonung
	to burn down (burnt, burnt) [ˌbɜːn ˈdaʊn]	verbrennen, abbrennen	
	best-selling [ˌbest ˈselɪŋ]	meistverkaufte/r/s	This is the best-selling brand.
4C	**fresh** [freʃ]	frisch	fresh bread ↔ stale bread
	manufacturing process [ˌmænjuˈfæktʃərɪŋ prəʊses]	Fertigungsverfahren, Herstellungsprozess	
	urgent [ˈɜːdʒənt]	dringend, eilig	The message is urgent!
	by air [baɪ ˈeə]	auf dem Luftweg	
	amazing [əˈmeɪzɪŋ]	erstaunlich	an amazing story – an amazed look on his face
	jewellery [ˈdʒuːəlri]	Schmuck	jewellery → jewel → jeweller's (shop)
4D	**logistics** [ləˈdʒɪstɪks]	Logistik	
4E	**participle** [ˈpɑːtɪsɪpl]	Partizip	
	model plane [ˈmɒdl pleɪn]	Modellflugzeug	
4F	**Spain** [speɪn]	Spanien	
	architect [ˈɑːkɪtekt]	Architekt/in	! Aussprache
	statue [ˈstætʃuː]	Statue	
	liberty [ˈlɪbəti]	Freiheit	
	to give (gave, given) [ɡɪv]	schenken	
	independent [ˌɪndɪˈpendənt]	unabhängig	independent → independence
	war [wɔː]	Krieg	war ↔ peace
4G	**globalised** [ˈɡləʊbəlaɪzd]	globalisiert	
4H	**thousand** [ˈθaʊznd]	tausend, Tausend	
	consequence [ˈkɒnsɪkwəns]	Folge, Auswirkung	! Betonung

Grammar summary | Skills files |  Vocabulary

	conditions [kən'dɪʃnz]	Bedingungen, Umstände	Conditions on the road are bad because of the snow.
	environment [ɪn'vaɪrənmənt]	Umwelt	
	locally ['ləʊkəli]	vor Ort	locally ↔ globally
5A	survey ['sɜːveɪ]	Umfrage	They are doing a survey of teenagers.
	graph [grɑːf]	Diagramm	
	overseas [ˌəʊvə'siːz]	in Übersee	She lived overseas for many years.
5B	toothpaste ['tuːθpeɪst]	Zahncreme	
	complicated ['kɒmplɪkeɪtɪd]	kompliziert	! Betonung
	Fairtrade ['feətreɪd]	Organisation für gerechten Handel	
V	pump [pʌmp]	Pumpe	
	to take sb to dinner [ˌteɪk tə 'dɪnə]	jdn zum Essen einladen	I'd like to take you to dinner tonight.
	Italian [ɪ'tæljən]	italienisch	

Unit 5 A month in New Zealand

1A	island ['aɪlənd]	Insel	! Die erste Silbe wird wie eye ausgesprochen.
	opportunity [ˌɒpə'tjuːnəti]	Gelegenheit, Chance	If I go to London, I'll have the opportunity to speak English.
	practise ['præktɪs]	üben, trainieren	
2A	Kiwi ['kiːwiː]	Neuseeländer/in; Kiwi (Vogelart; Frucht)	
	to cross [krɒs]	überqueren, kreuzen	Let's cross the road.
	paragraph ['pærəgrɑːf]	Absatz	
	New Zealander [ˌnjuː 'ziːləndə]	Neuseeländer/in	
	nickname ['nɪkneɪm]	Spitzname	
	to discover [dɪ'skʌvə]	entdecken	Columbus discovered America.
	explorer [ɪk'splɔːrə]	Entdecker/in	
	captain ['kæptɪn]	Kapitän	She is captain of the sports team.
	which is why [ˌwɪtʃ ɪz 'waɪ]	weshalb	He is ill. Which is why he can't come.
	Maori ['maʊri]	Maori	
	per cent [pə 'sent]	Prozent	
	screen [skriːn]	(Kino-)Leinwand	
	on screen [ɒn 'skriːn]	auf der Leinwand, im Kino	She is different on screen to in real life.
	lake [leɪk]	See	lake, mountain, river
	to film [fɪlm]	(Film) drehen	
	Lord Of The Rings [ˌlɔːd əv ðə 'rɪŋz]	Herr der Ringe (Buch- u. Filmtitel)	
	sports [spɔːts]	Sport	
	skiing ['skiːɪŋ]	Skifahren	
	surfing ['sɜːfɪŋ]	Surfen	
	dramatic [drə'mætɪk]	dramatisch, spektakulär	The end of the film was very dramatic.
	Auckland ['ɔːklənd]	Stadt in Neuseeland	
	however [haʊ'evə]	allerdings, jedoch	I didn't want to see the film. However, I enjoyed it.
	Wellington ['welɪŋtən]	Hauptstadt Neuseelands	
	accent ['æksent]	Akzent	The kids laughed at Susan's Scottish accent.
	jandals ['dʒændlz]	(NewZE:) Flip-Flops	(BE:) flip-flops
	barbie ['bɑːbi]	(NewZE:) Grillparty	
	barbecue ['bɑːbɪkjuː]	Grillparty	
2B	inhabitant [ɪn'hæbɪtənt]	Einwohner/in, Bewohner/in	How many inhabitants does Cologne have?
3B	pancake ['pænkeɪk]	Pfannkuchen	
	delicious [dɪ'lɪʃəs]	köstlich	Mmm! This cake is delicious.
	Here you are. [ˌhɪə ju 'ɑː]	(Hier,) bitte sehr.	
	I'm afraid … [aɪm ə'freɪd]	leider	I'm afraid I can't come tonight.
	absolutely ['æbsəluːtli]	absolut, ganz und gar	You're absolutely right!
	to be full up [bi ˌfʊl 'ʌp]	satt sein	I'm full up. I can't eat any more.
	at night [ət 'naɪt]	abends, nachts	at night ↔ during the day

	blanket [ˈblæŋkɪt]	Decke	It's cold. Can I have another blanket?
	How are you? [ˌhaʊ ə ˈjuː]	Wie geht es dir / Ihnen?	
	togs [tɒgz]	(NewZE:) Badeanzug	
	pardon [ˈpɑːdn]	Entschuldigung, Verzeihung	Pardon? Could you say that again?
	swimsuit [ˈswɪmsjuːt]	Badeanzug	
3F	soup [suːp]	Suppe	
	dessert [dɪˈzɜːt]	Nachtisch	! dessert ≠ desert (Wüste)
	to borrow [ˈbɒrəʊ]	leihen, ausleihen, borgen	Can I borrow your bike for the afternoon?
	flightless [ˈflaɪtləs]	flugunfähig	-less ↔ -ful: helpless ↔ helpful
4D	roast [rəʊst]	gebraten	
	beef [biːf]	Rind(fleisch)	
	pudding [ˈpʊdɪŋ]	Nachtisch	= dessert
4E	mediation [ˌmiːdiˈeɪʃn]	Vermittlung	
	interpreter [ɪnˈtɜːprɪtə]	Dolmetscher/in	
	salad [ˈsæləd]	Salat	Would you like mixed salad or potato salad?
	pillow [ˈpɪləʊ]	Kopfkissen	
4F	airhead [ˈeəhed]	Schwachkopf	
	loads (of) [ləʊdz]	massenhaft, jede Menge	= lots of
4G	explanation [ˌekspləˈneɪʃn]	Erläuterung, Erklärung	explanation → to explain
	grade [greɪd]	Note	
	average [ˈævərɪdʒ]	durchschnittlich	I got an average grade – not high but not low.
	satisfactory [ˌsætɪsˈfæktəri]	zufriedenstellend, befriedigend	
	sufficient [səˈfɪʃnt]	ausreichend, hinreichend	My grades are sufficient to get into college.
	poor [pʊə]	schlecht	
	unsatisfactory [ʌnˌsætɪsˈfæktəri]	unbefriedigend	My results were unsatisfactory. I must do the test again.
	to fail [feɪl]	durchfallen, (Prüfung) nicht bestehen	
5A	to divide [dɪˈvaɪd]	teilen	The teacher divided the class into two groups.
	currency [ˈkʌrənsi]	Währung	
	geography [dʒiˈɒgrəfi]	Geographie	The geography of the country played an important role in its history.
	entertainment [ˌentəˈteɪnmənt]	Unterhaltung	
V	journey [ˈdʒɜːni]	Fahrt	It's a long journey. It takes 12 hours.

Unit 6 Apprenticeships

	apprenticeship [əˈprentɪʃɪp]	Lehre, Lehrstelle	to do an apprenticeship
1A	exam [ɪgˈzæm]	Prüfung, Examen	
	to take an exam [ˌteɪk ən ɪgˈzæm]	eine Prüfung ablegen	to pass an exam
	GCSE (General Certificate of Secondary Education) [ˌdʒiː siː es ˈiː]	Schulabschlussprüfung für 16-Jährige in England, Wales und Nordirland	
	basic [ˈbeɪsɪk]	grundlegend, Grund-	He has a basic knowledge of French.
	advice [ədˈvaɪs]	Ratschlag, Rat	advice → to advise
	to give sb advice [ˌgɪv ədˈvaɪs]	jdn beraten, jdn etw raten	
	in detail [ɪn ˈdiːteɪl]	ausführlich, detailliert	Please write to me about it in detail.
1B	straight away [ˌstreɪt əˈweɪ]	sogleich, unverzüglich	Please hurry! Come straight away!
	training [ˈtreɪnɪŋ]	Ausbildung	
2	government [ˈgʌvənmənt]	Regierung	government → to govern
	alongside [əˌlɒŋˈsaɪd]	neben	
	experienced [ɪkˈspɪəriənst]	erfahren	an experienced worker
	tradespeople [ˈtreɪdzpiːpl]	Handwerker, Geschäftsleute	
	wage [weɪdʒ]	Lohn	salary = Gehalt
	to study [ˈstʌdi]	lernen, studieren	
	minimum [ˈmɪnɪməm]	Mindest-	You should get a minimum of seven hours' sleep every night.
	holiday [ˈhɒlədeɪ]	Feiertag	

| Grammar summary | Skills files | **Vocabulary**

	hands-on [ˌhændz ˈɒn]	praktisch, praxisnah	
	research [rɪˈsɜːtʃ]	Forschung(en), Untersuchungen	She does a lot of research on the Internet.
	lifetime [ˈlaɪftaɪm]	Leben	
	ability [əˈbɪləti]	Fähigkeit, Können	His ability to communicate is good.
	therapy [ˈθerəpi]	Therapie, Behandlung	
	nursing [ˈnɜːsɪŋ]	Krankenpflege, Pflege	Nursing is not an easy job.
	agriculture [ˈægrɪkʌltʃə]	Landwirtschaft	
	database [ˈdeɪtəbeɪs]	Datenbank	All the research is kept on this database.
	to register [ˈredʒɪstə]	eintragen, anmelden	
	directly [dəˈrektli]	direkt	Don't ask me. Talk to her directly.
2B	**certificate** [səˈtɪfɪkət]	Zeugnis, Nachweis, Urkunde	
2C	**make-up artist** [ˌmeɪkʌp ˈɑːtɪst]	Visagist/in	Make-up artists work in the theatre.
	travel tour guide [ˈtrævl tʊə gaɪd]	Reiseleiter/in	
	developer [dɪˈveləpə]	Entwickler/in	developer → development → to develop
3A	**flight attendant** [ˌflaɪt əˈtendənt]	Flugbegleiter/in	
	traineeship [treɪˈniːʃɪp]	Ausbildung(splatz)	-ship: apprenticeship, friendship
	sales [seɪlz]	Verkauf, Vertrieb	
	further [ˈfɜːðə]	weitere/r/s	I have no further questions.
	personnel [ˌpɜːsəˈnel]	Personal	
	personnel manager [ˌpɜːsəˈnel mænɪdʒə]	Personalleiter/in	! Aussprache
	Turkey [ˈtɜːki]	Türkei	
	free time [ˌfriː ˈtaɪm]	Freizeit	= leisure
	primary school [ˈpraɪməri skuːl]	Grundschule	
	secondary school [ˈsekəndri skuːl]	weiterführende Schule	
	work experience [ˈwɜːk ɪkspɪəriəns]	Berufserfahrung	
	travel agent [ˈtrævl eɪdʒənt]	Reisekaufmann/-frau; Reisebüro	
	fluent [ˈfluːənt]	fließend	She speaks fluent Chinese.
	Turkish [ˈtɜːkɪʃ]	türkisch, Türkisch	
	mother tongue [ˈmʌðə tʌŋ]	Muttersprache	She lives in Germany, but her mother tongue is Turkish.
3B	**job interview** [ˈdʒɒb ɪntəvjuː]	Vorstellungsgespräch	
	singing group [ˈsɪŋɪŋ gruːp]	Gesangsensemble	
	concert [ˈkɒnsət]	Konzert	
	city hall [ˌsɪti ˈhɔːl]	Rathaus	
4A	**to work hard** [ˌwɜːk ˈhɑːd]	hart arbeiten, fleißig sein	
	mark [mɑːk]	Note	= grade
4B	**main clause** [ˌmeɪn ˈklɔːz]	Hauptsatz	
4C	**whole** [həʊl]	ganze/r/s	I want to see the whole film. I've only seen part of it.
	Beware of dog [bɪˌweər əv ˈdɒg]	Warnung vor dem Hunde	
	gate [geɪt]	Tor	To enter the park, you had to go through a gate.
4D	**to improve** [ɪmˈpruːv]	verbessern	
	past [pɑːst]	Vergangenheit	In the past, I used to eat chocolate every day. Not these days.
	requirement [rɪˈkwaɪəmənt]	Anforderung	
	aged [eɪdʒd]	im Alter von	They accept candidates aged 18 and over.
	single [ˈsɪŋgl]	alleinstehend	
	housework [ˈhaʊswɜːk]	Haushaltsarbeit(en)	I hate doing housework!
	on average [ɒn ˈævərɪdʒ]	im Durchschnitt, durchschnittlich	
	region [ˈriːdʒən]	Region, Gebiet	Which region of the country do you come from?
4E	**comprehensive school** [kɒmprɪˈhensɪv skuːl]	Gesamtschule	
	French [frentʃ]	französisch, Französisch	The French love good food.
	science [ˈsaɪəns]	Naturwissenschaft(en)	
	Ltd. [ˈlɪmɪtɪd]	GmbH	= Limited

4F	**beetle** [ˈbiːtl]	Käfer	
	aeroplane [ˈeərəpleɪn]	Flugzeug	= plane
5A	**layout** [ˈleɪaʊt]	Layout	
5B	**interviewer** [ˈɪntəvjuːə]	Person, die ein Vorstellungsgespräch mit einem Bewerber führt	The interviewer was very friendly.
V	**scary** [ˈskeəri]	unheimlich, furchteinflößend	
	episode [ˈepɪsəʊd]	Folge (einer Radio-/TV-Serie)	I must watch TV tonight. It's the last episode!

Unit 7 Starting work

1A	**industrial electrician** [ɪnˌdʌstriəl ɪlekˈtrɪʃn]	Industrieelektriker/in	
2A	**retail assistant** [ˈriːteɪl əsɪstənt]	Einzelhandelskauffrau/-mann	**!** Aussprache
	till [tɪl]	Registrierkasse	
	advertising [ˈædvətaɪzɪŋ]	Werbung	advertising → advertisement → to advertise
	window display [ˈwɪndəʊ dɪspleɪ]	Schaufensterauslage	
	domestic goods [dəˌmestɪk ˈɡʊdz]	Haushaltswaren	Domestic goods are things like washing machines, ovens, fridges.
	retail store [ˈriːteɪl stɔː]	Einzelhandelsgeschäft	
	to suggest [səˈdʒest]	vorschlagen	to suggest → suggestion
	aspect [ˈæspekt]	Aspekt, Seite	
	to operate sth [ˈɒpəreɪt]	etw bedienen	Do you know how to operate that machine?
	to display sth [dɪˈspleɪ]	etw ausstellen, etw präsentieren	
	attractive [əˈtræktɪv]	attraktiv, reizvoll	It's an attractive price. I'm going to buy it.
	display [dɪˈspleɪ]	Präsentation, Auslage	
	huge [hjuːdʒ]	riesengroß	The shop has a huge range of domestic goods.
	sort [sɔːt]	Sorte, Art	
	behind the scenes [bɪˌhaɪnd ðə ˈsiːnz]	hinter den Kulissen	She seemed very happy, but behind the scenes she wasn't happy at all.
	whatever [wɒtˈevə]	was (auch immer)	
	sale [seɪl]	Verkauf, Ausverkauf	In some places, the sale of alcohol on Sundays is not allowed.
	campaign [kæmˈpeɪn]	Kampagne, Aktion	
3	**although** [ɔːlˈðəʊ]	obwohl	I'll help you, although I'm very busy.
	may [meɪ]	können, dürfen, mögen	
	nervous [ˈnɜːvəs]	nervös, aufgeregt	People are usually nervous before an exam or an interview.
	wide awake [ˌwaɪd əˈweɪk]	hellwach	
	uniform [ˈjuːnɪfɔːm]	Uniform, Dienstkleidung	Would you like to wear a uniform at work?
	traffic [ˈtræfɪk]	Verkehr	
	first thing in the morning [fɜːst ˌθɪŋ ɪn ðə ˈmɔːnɪŋ]	früh am Morgen	I always drink a cup of tea first thing in the morning.
	to smile [smaɪl]	lächeln	
	to enter sth [ˈentə]	etw betreten	He entered the room with a smile on his face.
	on time [ɒn ˈtaɪm]	pünktlich	
	to take a deep breath [teɪk ə ˌdiːp ˈbreθ]	tief Luft holen	If you take a deep breath, it may help you to be calm.
	impression [ɪmˈpreʃn]	Eindruck	
	enthusiastic [ɪnˌθjuːziˈæstɪk]	begeistert, engagiert	She's an enthusiastic skier.
	to be afraid [bi əˈfreɪd]	Angst haben	
	stupid [ˈstjuːpɪd]	dumm, albern	Oh, dear. That was a stupid thing to say!
	reliable [rɪˈlaɪəbl]	zuverlässig	
	quality [ˈkwɒləti]	Eigenschaft	The quality of our products is high.
	to promise [ˈprɒmɪs]	versprechen	
	to trust [trʌst]	vertrauen	I believe him. I think we can trust him.
	to get on with sb [ˌget ˈɒn wɪð]	mit jdm zurechtkommen	
	co-worker [ˈkəʊwɜːkə]	Arbeitskollege/-in	It's very important to get on with your co-workers.

| Grammar summary | Skills files | **Vocabulary** |

	solution [sə'luːʃn]	Lösung	
3A	**change** [tʃeɪndʒ]	Veränderung	He's bored. He needs a change.
	writer ['raɪtə]	Verfasser/in, Autor/in	
	opinion [ə'pɪniən]	Meinung	In my opinion, that's a bad decision.
4D	**section** ['sekʃn]	Abteilung	
	department store [dɪ'pɑːtmənt stɔː]	Kaufhaus, Warenhaus	Go down this street, and you'll see the department store on the right.
	in-store ['ɪnstɔː]	hauseigen, intern	
	travel agency ['trævl eɪdʒənsi]	Reisebüro	travel agency → travel agent
	pleased [pliːzd]	zufrieden	
	one day [ˌwʌn 'deɪ]	eines Tages	One day I'm going to tell her what I really think.
	effort ['efət]	Mühe, Anstrengung	
	to put in a lot of effort [pʊt ˌɪn ə lɒt əv 'efət]	sich große Mühe geben, sich sehr anstrengen	If you put a lot of effort into the job, you may get a promotion.
4E	**network** ['netwɜːk]	Netzwerk	
	to enjoy doing sth [ɪn'dʒɔɪ]	etw gern tun	I enjoy listening to music after work.
4F	**to afford sth** [ə'fɔːd]	sich etw leisten (können)	
	to stand sth [stænd]	etw ertragen	I can't stand loud noise.
	vegetarian [ˌvedʒə'teəriən]	Vegetarier/in	
	there's no point in doing sth [ðeəz ˌnəʊ 'pɔɪnt ɪn]	es hat keinen Sinn, etw zu tun	If you won't get an interview, there's no point in preparing for it.
	closed [kləʊzd]	geschlossen	
4H	**motorway** ['məʊtəweɪ]	Autobahn	In some countries you pay to use the motorways.
	surprise [sə'praɪz]	Überraschung	
5A	**to get started** [ˌget 'stɑːtɪd]	anfangen, loslegen	Is everybody here? Right, let's get started.

Alphabetisches Vokabular

A
a couple of ein paar 27
ability Fähigkeit, Können 58
absolutely absolut, ganz und gar 50
accent Akzent 49
accurate genau 10
to act spielen, schauspielern 29
administrative Verwaltungs- 30
administrative assistant Verwaltungsassistent/in 10
adult Erwachsene/r 9
advertising Werbung 68
advice Ratschlag, Rat 57
aeroplane Flugzeug 64
to afford sth sich etw leisten (können) 74
aged im Alter von 63
agriculture Landwirtschaft 58
airhead Schwachkopf 54
alcoholic alkoholisch 23
all day den ganzen Tag lang 8
alongside neben 58
although obwohl 70
amazing erstaunlich 42
apprentice Auszubildende/r, Lehrling 27
apprenticeship Lehre, Lehrstelle 56
architect Architekt/in 43
arrival Ankunft 18
Asia Asien 37
aspect Aspekt, Seite 68
to assemble montieren, zusammenbauen 38
assembly Montage 39
at lunchtime mittags 8
at night abends, nachts 50
at the moment im Augenblick 30
attractive attraktiv, reizvoll 68
Auckland Stadt in Neuseeland 49
automatic automatisch 28
automatically automatisch 28
average durchschnittlich 54

B
background Hintergrund 7
badly schlecht 27
baggage Gepäck 18
baggage reclaim Gepäckausgabe 18
bakery Bäckerei 37
barbecue Grillparty 49
barbie (NewZE:) Grillparty 49
based on anhand von, basierend auf 15
basic grundlegend, Grund- 57
to be afraid Angst haben 70
to be full up satt sein 50
to be happy sich freuen 28
to be on sale erhältlich sein, zum Verkauf stehen 40

because of aufgrund von, wegen 32
beef Rind(fleisch) 53
beetle Käfer 64
beginning Anfang 8
behind the scenes hinter den Kulissen 68
Best wishes, (Brief:) Alles Gute 25
best-selling meistverkaufte/r/s 42
Beware of dog Warnung vor dem Hunde 62
blanket Decke 50
to board an Bord gehen 18
boarding card Bordkarte 17
to borrow leihen, ausleihen, borgen 51
bracket Klammer 12
bridge Brücke 28
building Gebäude 28
to burn down (burnt, burnt) verbrennen, abbrennen 42
business trip Geschäftsreise 17
by air auf dem Luftweg 42
by sea auf dem Seeweg 42

C
campaign Kampagne, Aktion 68
can Dose 30
captain Kapitän 48
careers advice centre Berufsberatung(szentrum) 15
caring fürsorglich 10
carpenter Zimmermann, Schreiner 8
catastrophe Katastrophe 42
central zentral 38
certificate Zeugnis, Nachweis, Urkunde 59
change Veränderung 71
to change a baby einem Baby die Windeln wechseln 10
chart Tabelle, Diagramm 9
cheaply billig 41
to check in einchecken 17
check-in Abfertigung 17
check-in desk Abfertigungsschalter 17
cheese Käse 37
chemicals Chemikalien 27
chemicals company Chemiebetrieb 27
children's playground Kinderspielplatz 20
chips (BE:) Pommes frites 14
chocolate Schokolade 37
city hall Rathaus 61
class trip Klassenfahrt 14
clerk Angestellte/r 17
clever intelligent, gescheit 13
closed geschlossen 74
to communicate kommunizieren 10
complicated kompliziert 45

comprehensive school Gesamtschule 64
concert Konzert 61
conditions Bedingungen, Umstände 44
conference Konferenz 15
connection Verbindung 20
consequence Folge, Auswirkung 44
co-worker Arbeitskollege/-in 71
CPU CPU 38
creative kreativ, schöpferisch 13
to cross überqueren, kreuzen 48
currency Währung 55
customs Zoll 18
customs check Zollkontrolle 18
customs officer Zollbeamter 18
Czech Republic Tschechische Republik 39

D
daily routine (routinemäßiger) Tagesablauf 15
database Datenbank 58
day-to-day tagesaktuell, alltäglich 10
to decorate tapezieren 14
definition Definition 19
delicious köstlich 50
delivery Lieferung 37
to depart abfliegen, abfahren 18
department store Kaufhaus, Warenhaus 73
departure Abflug, Abfahrt 18
departures Abflughalle, Terminal 18
dessert Nachtisch 51
developer Entwickler/in 59
directly direkt 58
to discover entdecken 48
dispatch Versand 30
to dispatch versenden 34
display Präsentation, Auslage 68
to display sth etw ausstellen, etw präsentieren 68
to divide teilen 55
DIY (Do-it-yourself) Heimwerken 28
DIY shop Baumarkt 28
domestic goods Haushaltswaren 68
dramatic dramatisch, spektakulär 48
dream Traum 15

E
effort Mühe, Anstrengung 73
electrical technician Elektriker/in 20
electronic elektronisch 34
to enjoy sth etw genießen 21
to enjoy doing sth etw gern tun 73
to enter sth etw betreten 70
entertainment Unterhaltung 55
enthusiastic begeistert, engagiert 70
entrance Eingang 30

| Grammar summary | Skills files | **Vocabulary**

environment Umwelt 44
episode Folge (einer Radio-/TV-Serie) 65
equipment Geräte, Ausrüstung, Ausstattung 20
euro Euro 41
exact genau 29
exactly genau 28
exam Prüfung, Examen 57
exciting aufregend, spannend 20
to expect erwarten 9
to expect sb to do sth von jdm erwarten, etw zu tun 9
experienced erfahren 58
explanation Erläuterung, Erklärung 54
explorer Entdecker/in 48
expression Ausdruck 33

F
facility Anlage, Einrichtung 35
factory manager Betriebsleiter/in, Werksleiter/in 35
to fail durchfallen, (Prüfung) nicht bestehen 54
fair Jahrmarkt 20
Fairtrade Organisation für gerechten Handel 45
fantastic großartig, fantastisch 9
farm Farm, Bauernhof 40
farmer Farmer/in, Bauer/Bäuerin 40
to feed füttern 10
to fill in ausfüllen 21
to film (Film) drehen 48
finally schließlich, endlich 23
first thing in the morning früh am Morgen 70
flat (BE:) Wohnung 14
flight attendant Flugbegleiter/in 60
flightless flugunfähig 51
fluent fließend 60
(the) following der/die/das folgende 35
free time Freizeit 60
French französisch, Französisch 64
fresh frisch 42
further weitere/r/s 60

G
gate Flugsteig, Gate 18
gate Tor 63
GCSE (General Certificate of Secondary Education) Schulabschlussprüfung für 16-Jährige in England, Wales und Nordirland 57
geography Geographie 55
to get on with sb mit jdm zurechtkommen 71
to get ready (got, got) sich bereitmachen 6
to get started anfangen, loslegen 75
to give (gave, given) schenken 43
to give a talk einen Vortrag halten 15

to give sb advice jdn beraten, jdn etw raten 57
global weltumspannend, global 36
globalisation Globalisierung 40
globalised globalisiert 44
government Regierung 58
grade Note 54
graph Diagramm 45
to grow (grew, grown) wachsen 28; (Pflanze:) anbauen 40
grower Bauer/Bäuerin, Pflanzer/in 40

H
hairdressing Friseur-, Friseurhandwerk 8
hands-on praktisch, praxisnah 58
hard drive Festplatte 38
hardly ever kaum (jemals) 17
head office Zentrale 28
heading Überschrift 18
helpline Hotline 40
Here you are. (Hier,) bitte sehr. 50
holiday Feiertag 58
home Haus, Wohnung, Zuhause 28
hometown Heimatstadt 14
housework Haushaltsarbeit(en) 63
How are you? Wie geht es dir/Ihnen? 50
however allerdings, jedoch 49
huge riesengroß 68
humour Humor 9

I
ideal ideal 20
I'm afraid ... leider 50
to import importieren 40
impression Eindruck 70
to improve verbessern 63
in detail ausführlich, detailliert 57
in full vollständig 22
to include einbeziehen, einschließen 23
independent unabhängig 43
India Indien 40
industrial electrician Industrieelektriker/in 67
industry Branche, Industrie 9
inhabitant Einwohner/in, Bewohner/in 49
in-store hauseigen, intern 73
interpreter Dolmetscher/in 53
interviewer Person, die ein Vorstellungsgespräch mit einem Bewerber führt 65
to introduce sb jdn vorstellen 15
Ireland Irland 38
island Insel 47
Italian italienisch 45
Italy Italien 37

J
jandals (NewZE:) Flip-Flops 49
Japan Japan 35
jewellery Schmuck 42
job interview Vorstellungsgespräch 61
journey Fahrt 55

K
Kenya Kenia 40
key Schlüssel 21
keyboard Tastatur 38
kind Art, Sorte 8
Kiwi Neuseeländer/in; Kiwi (Vogelart; Frucht) 48

L
label Etikett 37
laboratory Labor 27
lake See 48
layout Layout 65
liberty Freiheit 43
lifetime Leben 58
link Verbindung, Kontakt 15
to load laden, verladen 30
loads (of) massenhaft, jede Menge 54
locally vor Ort 44
location Ort, Standort 35
logistics Logistik 43
to look round sich umsehen 29
Lord Of The Rings Herr der Ringe (Buch- u. Filmtitel) 48
Ltd. GmbH 64

M
machine Gerät, Maschine 17
main clause Hauptsatz 62
to make sure sicherstellen, gewährleisten 10
make-up artist Visagist/in 59
managing director Geschäftsführer/in 35
to manufacture herstellen 38
manufacturer Hersteller, Fabrikant 28
manufacturing process Fertigungsverfahren, Herstellungsprozess 42
Maori Maori 48
mark Note 62
market Markt 40
marmalade Marmelade 37
match Spiel, Partie 32
maths Mathe(matik) 9
may können, dürfen, mögen 70
mediation Vermittlung 53
mine Bergwerk 41
minimum Mindest- 58
to mix mischen 30
model plane Modellflugzeug 43
mother tongue Muttersprache 60
motherboard Hauptplatine 38

motorway Autobahn 74
mouse, mice Maus, Mäuse 38

N

nervous nervös, aufgeregt 70
network Netzwerk 73
New Zealander Neuseeländer/in 48
Nice to meet you. Schön, Sie kennenzulernen. 29
nickname Spitzname 48
No smoking. Rauchen verboten. 14
non-smoking Nichtraucher- 20
to note sth (etw) beachten 20
notes Notizen 7
nurse Krankenschwester, Krankenpfleger 14
nursery Kindertagesstätte 10
nursery worker Kindergärtner/in, Erzieher/in 10
nursing Krankenpflege, Pflege 58

O

oil Öl 30
on average im Durchschnitt, durchschnittlich 63
on foot zu Fuß 20
on one's own allein 9
on screen auf der Leinwand, im Kino 48
on the one hand einerseits 41
on the other hand andererseits 41
on the telephone am Telefon 40
on time pünktlich 70
one day (irgendwann) einmal 14; eines Tages 73
onto auf 30
to open sich öffnen 32
to operate sth etw bedienen 68
opinion Meinung 71
opportunity Gelegenheit, Chance 47
opposite gegenüber 7
overseas in Übersee 45
to paint malen 14

P

paint Farbe 27
pancake Pfannkuchen 50
paragraph Absatz 48
pardon Entschuldigung, Verzeihung 50
part Rolle 25
participle Partizip 43
passenger Passagier 18
passport Pass, Reisepass 18
passport check Passkontrolle 18
passport officer Passbeamte/r 18
past Vergangenheit 63
pepperoni Peperoni 37
per cent Prozent 48
personnel Personal 60
personnel manager Personalleiter/in 60
to photocopy fotokopieren 10

pillow Kopfkissen 53
pilot Pilot/in 19
playground Spielplatz 20
PLC AG, Aktiengesellschaft 27
pleased zufrieden 73
Pleased to meet you. Schön, Sie kennenzulernen. Sehr angenehm. 29
poor arm 41
poor schlecht 54
postcard Postkarte 25
powder Pulver 30
practise üben, trainieren 47
primary school Grundschule 60
to print drucken, ausdrucken 10
prize Preis, Auszeichnung 13
process Prozess, Vorgang, Verfahren 28
to process verarbeiten 38
production Produktion 30
to promise versprechen 71
pudding Nachtisch 53
pump Pumpe 45
to put in a lot of effort sich große Mühe geben, sich sehr anstrengen 73

Q

quality Qualität 30
quality Eigenschaft 71
quality control Qualitätskontrolle 30
quite ziemlich, recht 27

R

raw materials Rohstoffe 30
region Region, Gebiet 63
to register eintragen, anmelden 58
registration Anmeldung 21
registration form Formular 21
reliable zuverlässig 71
report Bericht 32
requirement Anforderung 63
research Forschung(en), Untersuchungen 58
research and development Forschungs- und Entwicklungsabteilung 30
responsible verantwortungsbewusst 10
result Ergebnis 9
retail assistant Einzelhandelskauffrau/ -mann 68
retail store Einzelhandelsgeschäft 68
roast gebraten 53
robot Roboter 28
role-play Rollenspiel 25
to role-play in einem Rollenspiel darstellen 25
roller coaster Achterbahn 20
Russia Russland 28

S

safe sicher 10
safety Sicherheit 10
salad Salat 53
salary Gehalt 40

sale Verkauf, Ausverkauf 68
sales Verkauf, Vertrieb 60
satisfactorily zufriedenstellend 27
satisfactory zufriedenstellend, befriedigend 54
sausage Wurst 37
scary unheimlich, furchteinflößend 65
schedule (Termin-)Plan 35
science Naturwissenschaft(en) 64
screen (Kino-)Leinwand 48
seat Sitz 18
secondary school weiterführende Schule 60
section Abteilung 73
security check Sicherheitskontrolle 18
security officer Sicherheitsbeamte/r, -beauftragte/r 18
self-discipline Selbstdisziplin 9
sense Sinn 9
to service warten, instandhalten 20
sick krank 14
Silicon Valley Computerzentrum in Kalifornien 40
Singapore Singapur 39
singing group Gesangsensemble 61
single alleinstehend 63
skiing Skifahren 48
to smile lächeln 70
smoothly reibungslos, glatt 10
solution Lösung 71
sort Sorte, Art 68
soup Suppe 51
Spain Spanien 43
sports Sport 48
to stand sth etw ertragen 74
statue Statue 43
stay Aufenthalt 21
to store lagern, speichern 30
straight away sogleich, unverzüglich 57
to study lernen, studieren 58
stupid dumm, albern 70
sufficient ausreichend, hinreichend 54
to suggest vorschlagen 68
surfing Surfen 48
surprise Überraschung 74
survey Umfrage 45
swimsuit Badeanzug 50

T

to take a deep breath tief Luft holen 70
to take an exam eine Prüfung ablegen 57
to take sb to dinner jdn zum Essen einladen 45
talk Vortrag 15
tank Tank 30
telephone Telefon 10
test facility Versuchseinrichtung, Testanlage 35
test manager Versuchsleiter/in 35
That depends. Das kommt darauf an. 8

Anhang Vocabulary **133**

| Grammar summary | Skills files | **Vocabulary**

theme park Vergnügungs-, Themenpark 20
therapy Therapie, Behandlung 58
there's no point in doing sth es hat keinen Sinn, etw zu tun 74
this way hier entlang 29
thousand tausend, Tausend 44
through durch (… hindurch) 18
till Registrierkasse 68
togs (NewZE:) Badeanzug 50
tonne Tonne 42
toothpaste Zahncreme 45
total Gesamtanzahl 21
tour Rundgang, Tour 30
tourism Tourismus 40
tower Turm 38
tractor Traktor 28
tradespeople Handwerker, Geschäftsleute 58
traffic Verkehr 70
to train to be sb eine Ausbildung zum/zur … machen 8
trainee Auszubildende/r 8
traineeship Ausbildung(splatz) 60
trainer Ausbilder/in 27
training Ausbildung 57
tram Straßenbahn, Tram 17
travel agency Reisebüro 73
travel agent Reisekaufmann/-frau; Reisebüro 60
travel tour guide Reiseleiter/in 59
to trust vertrauen 71
Turkey Türkei 60
Turkish türkisch, Türkisch 60
to type tippen 10

U
uniform Uniform, Dienstkleidung 70
unit Einheit 38
unsatisfactory unbefriedigend 54
up there da oben 30
urgent dringend, eilig 42

V
vase Vase 42
vegetarian Vegetarier/in 74

W
wage Lohn 58
war Krieg 43
warehouse Lager 30
Wellington Hauptstadt Neuseelands 49
whatever was (auch immer) 68
which is why weshalb 48
whole ganze/r/s 62
wide awake hellwach 70
Wi-Fi drahtlos, wireless 20
window display Schaufensterauslage 68
wood Holz 8
woodworking Holzbe-/-verarbeitung, Holz- 8
work experience Berufserfahrung 60
to work hard hart arbeiten, fleißig sein 62
writer Verfasser/in, Autor/in 71

Bildquellennachweis

4.1 iStockphoto (MachineHeadz), Calgary, Alberta; **4.2** iStockphoto (René Mansi), Calgary, Alberta; **4.3** iStockphoto (Tony Tremblay), Calgary, Alberta; **4.4** Mauritius Images (Alamy), Mittenwald; **4.5** iStockphoto (Jeanniemay), Calgary, Alberta; **5.1** iStockphoto (Sturti), Calgary, Alberta; **5.2** shutterstock (Lisa F. Young), New York, NY; **5.3** iStockphoto (Kyoshino), Calgary, Alberta; **5.4** shutterstock (George Dolgikh), New York, NY; **6.1** iStockphoto (MachineHeadz), Calgary, Alberta; **6.2** shutterstock (Cynthia Farmer), New York, NY; **8.1** Fotolia.com (Lightpoet), New York; **8.2** shutterstock (Auremar), New York, NY; **9** iStockphoto (Machine Headz), Calgary, Alberta; **10.1** shutterstock (StockLite), New York, NY; **10.2** iStockphoto (Omgimages), Calgary, Alberta; **11** iStockphoto (Dean Drobot), Calgary, Alberta; **13** iStockphoto (Diego Cervo), Calgary, Alberta; **14.1**; **14.5** iStockphoto (Kali Nine LLC), Calgary, Alberta; **14.2** iStockphoto (MartinPrescott), Calgary, Alberta; **14.3** iStockphoto (Susanna Fieramosca Naranjo), Calgary, Alberta; **14.4** iStockphoto (Andrew Howe), Calgary, Alberta; **14.6** iStockphoto (Jmalov), Calgary, Alberta; **15** Klett-Archiv, Stuttgart; **16.1** iStockphoto (René Mansi), Calgary, Alberta; **16.2** iStockphoto (Neustockimages), Calgary, Alberta; **18.1** iStockphoto (Quavondo), Calgary, Alberta; **18.2** iStockphoto (Matjaz Boncina), Calgary, Alberta; **18.3** Keystone (Volkmar Schulz), Hamburg; **20.1** iStockphoto (davidf), Calgary, Alberta; **20.2** Thinkstock (iStockphoto), München; **20.3** shutterstock (Kevin Eaves), New York, NY; **21** iStockphoto (Jeffrey Smith), Calgary, Alberta; **22.1** Thinkstock (Photodisc), München; **22.2** Fotolia.com (Nicemonkey), New York; **22.3** Thinkstock (Creatas), München; **24** Thinkstock (Goodshoot), München; **25** ©Collins DVD/AudioCD/Book ISBN 978-0-00-743199-1; **26.1** Klett-Archiv (A. Raftaki), Stuttgart; **26.2** iStockphoto (Tony Tremblay), Calgary, Alberta; **28.1** shutterstock (Zastol`skiy Victor Leonidovich), New York, NY; **28.2** shutterstock (Joe Gough), New York, NY; **28.3** shutterstock (NanoStock), New York, NY; **28.4** GOODSHOOT (Goodshoot), Annecy-Le-Vieux; **29** Klett-Archiv (A. Raftaki), Stuttgart; **30.1** Mauritius Images (Hans-Peter Merten), Mittenwald; **30.2** shutterstock (Elena Moiseeva), New York, NY; **31.1** iStockphoto (Jacom Stephens), Calgary, Alberta; **31.2** shutterstock (Rezachka), New York, NY; **31.3** JupiterImages photos.com (photos.com), Tucson, AZ; **31.4** Fotolia.com (Goodluz), New York; **31.5** JupiterImages photos.com (Photos.com), Tucson, AZ; **33** Thinkstock (Stockbyte), München; **35** ©Collins DVD/AudioCD/Book ISBN 978-0-00-743199-1; **36.1** Mauritius Images (Alamy), Mittenwald; **36.2** Fotolia.com (Art Allianz), New York; **38** Thinkstock (Monkey Business), München; **39.1** PantherMedia GmbH (Marc Dietrich), München; **39.2** Dell GmbH, Frankfurt; **39.3** iStockphoto (PhotoTalk), Calgary, Alberta; **39.4**; **39.8** MEV Verlag GmbH, Augsburg; **39.5** shutterstock (Wallenrock), New York, NY; **39.6** shutterstock (Péter Gudella), New York, NY; **39.7** Thinkstock (SisterF), München; **40.1** BigStockPhoto.com (Darrenmbaker), Davis, CA; **40.2** iStockphoto (AnkNet), Calgary, Alberta; **40.3** iStockphoto (Bryan Smith), Calgary, Alberta; **41** Böthling, Jörg/visualindia.de (Boethling), Hamburg; **43** shutterstock (Magmarcz), New York, NY; **44** iStockphoto (Panchof), Calgary, Alberta; **45** TransFair e.V. (Harald Gruber), Köln; **45** ©Collins DVD/AudioCD/Book ISBN 978-0-00-743199-1; **46.1** Fotolia.com (Goodluz), New York; **46.2** iStockphoto (Jeanniemay), Calgary, Alberta; **48.1** Fotolia.com (Braden Gunem), New York; **48.2** Fotolia.com (ALCE), New York; **48.3** ddp images GmbH (defd movies/Herr der Ringe, Der - Teil 3: Die Rückkehr des Königs), Hamburg; **48.4** Corbis (Christian Liewig/Liewig Media Sports), Düsseldorf; **49** shutterstock (NZGMW), New York, NY; **53.1** shutterstock (Julie Keen), New York, NY; **53.2** Avenue Images GmbH (Banana Stock), Hamburg; **55** shutterstock, New York, NY; **55** ©Collins DVD/AudioCD/Book ISBN 978-0-00-743199-1; **56.1** iStockphoto (Sturti), Calgary, Alberta; **56.2** Fotolia.com (Goodluz), New York; **56.3** iStockphoto (Goodluz), Calgary, Alberta; **58.1**; **58.2** iStockphoto (BartCo), Calgary, Alberta; **59.1** Fotolia.com (Contrastwerkstatt), New York; **59.2** Getty Images RF (Tim Hall/Digital Vision), München; **59.3** iStockphoto (Chris Schmidt), Calgary, Alberta; **60** Klett-Archiv (A. Raftaki), Stuttgart; **61.1** Klett-Archiv (A. Raftaki), Stuttgart; **61.2** iStockphoto (Csondy), Calgary, Alberta; **62.1** Corel Corporation Deutschland, Unterschleissheim; **62.2** iStockphoto (Adam Booth), Calgary, Alberta; **62.3** iStockphoto (Lance Bellers), Calgary, Alberta; **62.4** iStockphoto (Maytals), Calgary, Alberta; **62.5** Fotolia.com (Jerome Dancette), New York; **63** Thinkstock (Comstock), München; **64** Fotolia.com (Denise Kappa), New York; **65** Klett-Archiv, Stuttgart; **66.1** shutterstock (Lisa F. Young), New York, NY; **66.2** Thinkstock (monkeybusinessimages), München; **68.1** Avenue Images GmbH (Juice Images), Hamburg; **68.2** iStockphoto (OJO_Images), Calgary, Alberta; **68.3** iStockphoto (Fatihhoca), Calgary, Alberta; **68.4** iStockphoto (Fotofrog), Calgary, Alberta; **68.5** iStockphoto (Anna Rise), Calgary, Alberta; **68.6** iStockphoto (Hh5800), Calgary, Alberta; **68.7** shutterstock (Milkos), New York, NY; **70** iStockphoto (Georgijevic), Calgary, Alberta; **71** iStockphoto (Mediaphotos), Calgary, Alberta; **73** Fotolia.com (Minerva Studio), New York; **74** iStockphoto (Blende64),

Calgary, Alberta; **74** iStockphoto (DaveLongMedia), Calgary, Alberta; **75** Klett-Archiv, Stuttgart; **76** iStockphoto (Kyoshino), Calgary, Alberta; **78** iStockphoto (Kupicoo), Calgary, Alberta; **79** iStockphoto (Image Source), Calgary, Alberta; **80.1** shutterstock (michaeljung), New York, NY; **80.2** shutterstock (juniart), New York, NY; **82** dreamstime.com (Nyul), Brentwood, TN; **84** iStockphoto (Vigold), Calgary, Alberta; **86** iStockphoto (Ussr), Calgary, Alberta; **87** iStockphoto (GlobalStock), Calgary, Alberta; **88** dreamstime.com (Nyul), Brentwood, TN; **88** shutterstock (Ficus777), New York, NY; **90** Avenue Images GmbH (Juice Images), Hamburg; **91** shutterstock (Colorlife), New York, NY; **92.1** shutterstock (Edyta Pawlowska), New York, NY; **92.2** Fotolia.com (Pkchai), New York; **95** iStockphoto (GoodLifeStudio), Calgary, Alberta; **96** shutterstock (George Dolgikh), New York, NY; **120** Klett-Archiv, Stuttgart; **COVER** Thinkstock (Comstock), München

Sollte es in einem Einzelfall nicht gelungen sein, den korrekten Rechteinhaber ausfindig zu machen, so werden berechtigte Ansprüche selbstverständlich im Rahmen der üblichen Regelungen abgegolten.